WRITERS AND THEIR WORK

ISOBEL ARMSTRONG
Consultant Editor

LEWIS GRASSIC GIBBON

LEWIS GRASSIC GIBBON

William K Malcolm

© Copyright 2023 by William K Malcolm

First published in 2020 by
Liverpool University Press
4 Cambridge Street
Liverpool L69 7ZU

This paperback edition published 2023

on behalf of
Northcote House Publishers Ltd
Mary Tavy
Devon PL19 9PY

The right of William K Malcolm to be identified as the author of this book has been asserted by him in accordance with the Copyright, Design and Patents Act 1988. All rights reserved. No part of this book may be reproduced, stored in a retrieval system, or transmitted, in any form or by any means, electronic, mechanical, photocopying, recording, or otherwise, without the prior written permission of the publisher.

British Library Cataloguing-in-Publication Data
A catalogue record for this book is available from the British Library

ISBN 978-1-7896-2062-7 (hardback)
ISBN 978-1-78962-063-4 (paperback)

Typeset by Carnegie Book Production, Lancaster

In memory of
RHEA MARTIN
1931–2014

Contents

Acknowledgements		ix
Biographical Outline		xi
Abbreviations		xv
Note on the Texts		xvii
1	Life and Background	1
2	Narrative Preludes: *The Calends of Cairo* and *Persian Dawns, Egyptian Nights*	17
3	The Real Stuff of History: *Hanno, Niger, The Conquest of the Maya* and *Nine Against the Unknown*	25
4	Autofiction: *Stained Radiance* and *The Thirteenth Disciple*	39
5	Setting Tales upon the Truth: *Three Go Back, The Lost Trumpet* and *Gay Hunter*	49
6	Haunted by Horrors: *Image and Superscription* and *Spartacus*	59
7	Distant Cousin Lewis Grassic Gibbon: *A Scots Quair* (*Sunset Song, Cloud Howe* and *Grey Granite*) and *Scottish Scene*	69
8	Legacy	127
Notes		141

Bibliography	149
Further Reading	155
Index	157

Acknowledgements

In the course of four decades of dedicated research on James Leslie Mitchell/Lewis Grassic Gibbon I have amassed a host of debts to the good folk who have assisted me in my work. I should like to mention in particular the editors and publishers who have previously printed my ideas on Mitchell, and Northcote House and Liverpool University Press who in accepting the present volume for their prestigious Writers and their Work series enabled me to gain a balanced perspective on my forthcoming biography of Mitchell; Isabella Williamson at the Grassic Gibbon Centre in Mitchell's renowned heartland of Arbuthnott; and Aberdeen University Library, Edinburgh University Library Special Collections, the Mitchell Library in Glasgow and the Trustees of the National Library of Scotland, together with the Estate of James Leslie Mitchell, for granting permission to quote from manuscript material. Thanks are due also to the Grassic Gibbon Centre for providing photographs of Mitchell from their unique family archive. Pre-eminently, however, I remain indebted to Leslie Mitchell's family for their unflagging encouragement and assistance over the years: Ray Mitchell, the most loyal guardian of her husband's legacy; her daughter Rhea Martin, who assumed her mother's mantle with due sympathy and diligence; and her son Daryll Mitchell, who in his consideration and generosity personified many of his parents' outstanding qualities.

James Leslie Mitchell/Lewis Grassic Gibbon at Bloomfield
Photograph © The Grassic Gibbon Centre

Biographical Outline

1901	James Leslie Mitchell born at noon on 13 February at Hillhead of Seggat, Auchterless, Aberdeenshire to James McIntosh Mitchell and his wife, née Lilias Grant Gibbon.
1907	March–May: education at Auchterless Public School.
1907–08	Mitchell family resident in Aberdeen; attends King Street School.
1908	May: Mitchells move to croft of Bloomfield, Arbuthnott, Kincardineshire, in the Mearns; admitted to Arbuthnott Parish School.
1916–17	attends Mackie Academy, Stonehaven.
1917–19	reporter with *The Aberdeen Daily Journal*.
1919	January–June: junior reporter on *The Scottish Farmer* in Glasgow; summer: recuperation at Bloomfield after nervous breakdown, following dismissal from job for falsifying business expenses.
1919–23	service as clerk in Royal Army Service Corps, in Baghdad (March–September 1920); Jerusalem (November 1921–February 1922); Cairo (February 1922–February 1923).
1923	April–August: spends summer as recluse at Bloomfield; August: enlists as clerk in Royal Air Force.
1924	18 October: first published story, 'Siva Plays the Game', appears in *T.P.'s and Cassell's Weekly*.
1925	15 August: marries Rebecca Middleton (later Ré, Rhea or Ray) at Fulham Registry Office; August: posted to RAF Kenley, Surrey; settles with wife in Kenley.

1926	January–February: Ray convalescent at Purley Cottage Hospital following serious miscarriage; June: transferred to Uxbridge; September: Mitchells move to Harrow, Middlesex.
1927	December: stationed at RAF Upavon, Wiltshire; Mitchells move to Shepherd's Bush, London W12.
1928	June: publication of first book, *Hanno: or The Future of Exploration*, by Kegan Paul, Trench, Trubner and Co. Ltd, London.
1929	January: publication of 'For Ten's Sake', first of series of short stories to appear in *The Cornhill Magazine*.
1930	14 March: final discharge from RAF; 17 March: birth of daughter, Rhea Sylvia Leslie Mitchell; September: publication of first novel, *Stained Radiance: A Fictionist's Prelude*, by Jarrolds, London; October: tries to establish Society of Militant Pacifists, anarchist political group dedicated to aim of abolishing war.
1931	applies twice, unsuccessfully, to join the Communist Party of Great Britain (CPGB); January: *The Thirteenth Disciple: Being Portrait and Saga of Malcom Maudslay in his Adventure Through the Dark Corridor* published by Jarrolds; July: *The Calends of Cairo*, Introduced by Mr. H.G. Wells and Dr. Leonard Huxley, published by Jarrolds, published as *Cairo Dawns: A Story Cycle with a Proem* by the Bobbs-Merrill Company, Indianapolis; December: Mitchells move to Welwyn Garden City, Hertfordshire.
1932	January: *Three Go Back* published by Jarrolds and by Bobbs-Merrill, Indianapolis; July: *The Lost Trumpet* published by Jarrolds and by Bobbs-Merrill; August: *Sunset Song: A Novel*, first work published under Scots pseudonym of Lewis Grassic Gibbon, published as first volume of *A Scots Quair* trilogy by Jarrolds; November: *Persian Dawns, Egyptian Nights*, with a Foreword by J.D. Beresford, published by Jarrolds.
1933	March: *Image and Superscription: A Novel* published by Jarrolds; May: Lewis Grassic Gibbon, *Cloud Howe*, second book of *A Scots Quair*, published by Jarrolds; August: *Spartacus* published by Jarrolds.

1934	February: *Niger: The Life of Mungo Park* published under pen name of Lewis Grassic Gibbon by The Porpoise Press, Edinburgh and *The Conquest of the Maya*, with a Foreword by Professor G. Elliot Smith, published by Jarrolds; 16 March: birth of son, Daryll Allan Leslie Mitchell; May: *Gay Hunter* published by William Heinemann; June: publication of Hugh MacDiarmid and Lewis Grassic Gibbon, *Scottish Scene: or The Intelligent Man's Guide to Albyn* by Jarrolds; November: Lewis Grassic Gibbon, *Grey Granite*, final part of *A Scots Quair*, published by Jarrolds and J. Leslie Mitchell and Lewis Grassic Gibbon, *Nine Against the Unknown: A Record of Geographical Exploration* published by Jarrolds, published under sole authorship of Mitchell as *Earth Conquerors: The Lives and Achievements of the Great Explorers* by Simon and Schuster Inc., New York; December: suffers acute stomach pains, diagnosed as gastritis.
1935	4 February: undergoes operation at Queen Victoria Hospital, Welwyn, for perforated gastric ulcer; 7 February: James Leslie Mitchell/Lewis Grassic Gibbon dies, age thirty-three years and eleven months.

Abbreviations

CC	*The Calends of Cairo*
CH	*Cloud Howe*
CM	*The Conquest of the Maya*
GG	*Grey Granite*
GH	*Gay Hunter*
H	*Hanno: or The Future of Exploration*
IS	*Image and Superscription*
LT	*The Lost Trumpet*
N	*Niger: The Life of Mungo Park*
NAU	*Nine Against the Unknown: A Record of Geographical Exploration*
NLS	National Library of Scotland, Edinburgh
PDEN	*Persian Dawns, Egyptian Nights*
S	*Spartacus*
ScSc	*Scottish Scene: or The Intelligent Man's Guide to Albyn*
Sm	*Smeddum: A Lewis Grassic Gibbon Anthology*, **edited by** Valentina Bold
SR	*Stained Radiance*
SS	*Sunset Song*
TD	*The Thirteenth Disciple*
TGB	*Three Go Back*

Note on the Texts

While the works published under the pen name of Lewis Grassic Gibbon are his most famous, unlike Eric Arthur Blair, whose literary career was exclusively pursued under the moniker of George Orwell, Leslie Mitchell's publishing history encompassed divided authorship. This being the case, for simplicity's sake throughout this study reference will be made to Leslie Mitchell generically under his real name. Textual references are to the most widely available modern reprints, principally those belonging to Polygon's enterprising Lewis Grassic Gibbon Series that has brought back *Stained Radiance, Three Go Back, Persian Dawns, Egyptian Nights, The Lost Trumpet, Spartacus* and *Nine Against the Unknown* as well as the miscellany *The Speak of the Mearns*. These volumes boast perceptive introductions by Professor Ian Campbell. Polygon also republished *Gay Hunter*, with an incisive introduction by Edwin Morgan. Page references to *The Thirteenth Disciple* follow the paperback edition brought out by B&W Publishing in 1995. The *Polychromata* story cycle and other English stories from *The Cornhill Magazine* and *The Millgate Monthly* are cited in the more polished book versions revised by Mitchell himself for the collections *The Calends of Cairo* and *Persian Dawns, Egyptian Nights*, the latter of which is available from Polygon in a photographic reprint of the first edition.

References to the trilogy *A Scots Quair* are to the most reliable modern texts: *Sunset Song*, introduced by Ali Smith and edited by the present writer for Penguin Classics in 2007; and *Cloud Howe* and *Grey Granite*, edited by Thomas Crawford for Canongate Books in 1988 and 1990. The secondary Grassic Gibbon pieces, including the essays and stories first published in *Scottish Scene* together with a comprehensive sample of Mitchell's early stories, poems and typescripts, are most easily found in the miscellany

Smeddum: A Lewis Grassic Gibbon Anthology edited by Valentina Bold for Canongate in 2001, which also contains the unfinished novel edited by Ian Campbell and published by the Ramsay Head Press in 1982 as *The Speak of the Mearns*. For ease of access all references to these secondary works use this volume.

In 2020 the National Library of Scotland made pdf files of the first editions of all of Mitchell's books barring *Scottish Scene* available to download from their website, at https://digital.nls.uk/lewis-grassic-gibbon-books/archive/205174226.

1

Life and Background

More than eighty years after James Leslie Mitchell's early death the time is ripe for the fresh appraisal of a figure who combines literary acclaim with a popularity in Scotland unsurpassed by any writer, a writer who is now a household name ranking alongside that of Robert Burns the national bard. Widely studied in secondary schools, repeatedly voted the nation's best novelist by the reading public and famously hailed as author of First Minister Nicola Sturgeon's favourite book *Sunset Song*, Mitchell's status in Scotland as one of the foremost writers of modern times, particularly under the more popular alias of Lewis Grassic Gibbon, is assured. Long recognised as a seminal force in modern Scottish literature, Mitchell is now universally perceived as a writer of world repute. Critics at home and, increasingly, on the continent have categorically established his importance on several fronts, with *A Scots Quair*, the epic trilogy from the early 1930s, earning a global standing that in the twenty-first century can comfortably be adjudged canonical.

Leslie Mitchell's literary reputation is poignantly bound up with his astonishing life story, tracing the tragedy of a humble crofter's son dying at a desperately young age while poised on the brink of world-wide celebrity. His short life exerts its own fascination as a mercurial narrative marked by all sorts of dramatic spikes and troughs. His was a unique personality forged by a remarkable combination of personal circumstances; he was also very much a child of the dramatic times that he lived through. Born on 13 February 1901, less than a month after the death of Queen Victoria, Leslie Mitchell's life neatly chronicled the opening decades of the twentieth century. In his second novel *The Thirteenth Disciple* metafictionally Mitchell places himself firmly within the zeitgeist of post-Victorian Britain. The opening chapter ends with one of the key passages in Mitchell's whole corpus, as a huge bonfire set alight in the homeland of the autobiographical protagonist Malcom Maudslay at midnight on New Year's Eve in 1900 is represented as a raging conflagration that ushers in the new age and that the author hails in symbolic terms proclaiming his novel's modernity:

> They were burning out the nineteenth century: Victorian England, Victorian Europe, cant a religion, smugness a creed, gods in whiskers and morals in stays … . That fire went up with the crackling of crinolines and bustles, brothels and bethels. It screamed with the agony of murdered children in Midland factories, soughed and glimmered in a wind of such pious belching as no other century had ever seen. It flamed on a gaseous literature and an idiot art, sank and seethed and roared again with the fuel of gutter dreams and palace spites. Christianity and nationalism, socialism and individualism – they flared and broke and showered the dark hillsides with glowing embers. (*TD*12)

Even at this formative stage in his writing career, in the motif denoting the cultural purgation of all things recondite Mitchell was formally signalling his repudiation of the Victorian values that had dominated his education and upbringing. Unlike the celebrations from the previous year commemorating the chronological change of century, the bonfire selected by Mitchell denotes the end of an era, transitioning from the Victorian to the Edwardian age. The dawn of a whole new historical epoch thus demanded a fresh artistic response analogous with the new social and intellectual order accompanying the war, and from his earliest fiction Mitchell accordingly displayed a propensity for experimentation with all sorts of non-realist fiction modes. At this time in 1931, though, the retrospective renunciation of the past hadn't yet given rise to a workable aesthetic attuned for the present, let alone one, as evolved by Grassic Gibbon, that was future-proofed by its transcendent originality.

Mitchell's own life experience was linked in with some of the most important happenings of modern times, and in fact he was an active participant in, and eye-witness to, the grand sweep of events that can be extrapolated as pivotal agents in the shaping of our own world: the depopulation of the countryside; the intensification of socially divisive capitalist economics; the left-wing factionalism immediately following the First World War leading up to the formation of the Communist Party of Great Britain (CPGB); the efforts of Britain and its allies to prosper globally from their victory in the war; the scramble by the West to exploit the natural resources possessed by territories in the Middle East; the crippling unemployment rampant between the wars; the upsurge of interest in Scottish political and cultural nationalism; the rise of totalitarianism, principally fascism. Mitchell's writing is a barometer of the times, but the precise nature of his literary achievement set against this dramatic geopolitical background has still to be adequately sketched. It's my intention to address these biographical and critical aims in this monograph.

Early on in his adolescence Mitchell rested his hopes for the future on a literary vocation, and a school essay records his burning ambition to find a career in journalism.[1] His background, though, did little to help him to chase this dream. While many working-class writers have benefited from a stimulating home environment where books and education were highly prized (often as a potential means of securing social advancement), Mitchell didn't even have access to the oral tradition recycling tales and ballads and folklore from bygone times that helped to form writers like Robert Burns, James Hogg and Sir Walter Scott. Family relationships in the rural Northeast up to comparatively recent times can be hard to pin down due to the social mobility that was a requirement of the semi-itinerant agricultural workforce and to the almost endemic prevalence of illegitimacy, but in Mitchell's case his genealogy is well documented. Both father James McIntosh Mitchell and mother Lilias (Lily) Grant Gibbon came from Northeast farming families whose lineage was traceable to the last decades of the seventeenth century, reaching almost as far back as written records exist. Both sides of the family were products of the farming economy historically persisting in rural Scotland into modern times, in an area of the Northeast memorably dubbed 'the poor man's country' in twin-edged tribute to the fortitude demanded of small-scale farmers to perpetuate a subsistence economy in a period when capitalist farming had become established as the dominant mode of agricultural production from the middle of the nineteenth century.[2] The smallholder's avowed autonomy came at a heavy price for the leasing of a rudimentary farmhouse with small outbuildings and three or four surrounding fields from a landowner driven by the profit motive. Even in clement years the combination of the restricted scale of the holdings (often totalling less than 50 acres), unfavourable rents, poor quality of land and primitive working conditions condemned the peasantry to a life of enduring poverty from which it was virtually impossible to escape, even given the whole family's collective commitment to the unremitting work schedule needed to keep the concern financially afloat. The Mitchells and the Gibbons were long-term victims of this harsh social ethos, as modest farmers historically documented at Insch, Strathdon and Kildrummy in the heart of Aberdeenshire. There's no record of any of Mitchell's ancestors managing to break free from the stifling cycle of poverty; Lily Gibbon's father George Gibbon was a farm servant, and indeed James Mitchell's illegitimacy, as the first son born to Isabella Mitchell, a lowly domestic servant, would only have been deleterious to his future social prospects.

The peculiarities of the Mitchell family dynamic fostered internal tensions that became increasingly unhappy for Leslie Mitchell. When James Mitchell married Lily Gibbon in Aberdeen on New Year's Eve in 1898, he was eleven years older than her but she already had two sons born to different fathers. George, born illegitimate at Lily's previous place of work, was then five years old; John, subject to a successful paternity suit in 1898 naming his father as a farm servant from Banchory, was an infant just a year old. Lily Gibbon showed admirable courage in asserting her rights to identify her second child's father in a society that was both hierarchical and patriarchal. Within the Mitchell family eldest brother George appeared the heir apparent by order of seniority but not by blood – a confusing situation resolved by his effective disappearance on his emigration to Canada in early adulthood. As far as the future writer was concerned, these circumstances fuelled one of the most common tropes of his fiction involving shocking genealogical twists. More practically, counterintuitively father James Mitchell overcompensated for taking on paternal responsibility for his wife's previous sons, treating George and John with demonstrably greater indulgence than his own child; the fractious relationship between father and his only begotten son lasted throughout their lifetime, with Lily Mitchell doomed to play eternal role of intermediary – although in true Northeast fashion obedience to her husband was paramount.

Mentored by Alexander Gray, his idealistic young teacher at Arbuthnott School destined to become his friend in later life, Leslie Mitchell showed a precocious facility with the written word, as evidenced by the surviving juvenilia of school essay jotters boasting ambitious stylistic techniques and dealing with an impressive range of subjects, from simple observations of local country scenes to reflections on history and current affairs, with the outbreak and progress of the war increasingly coming to the fore. Mitchell's literary prowess seemed to come from nowhere, widening the emotional gulf with his uncomprehending parents and prompting widespread bafflement among his peers and members of the greater farming community of Arbuthnott. In a world that was even less a creative meritocracy than modern-day Britain subsequently Mitchell persistently showed the courage of his convictions to earn his success the hard way, by virtue of his own prodigious abilities and stupendous industry; along the way he had to endure years of frustration and disappointment – sometimes self-inflicted – before he could settle down to his chosen vocation of what he termed 'a professional writer-cratur'.[3]

The most authoritative formal definition of the peasant and the peasantry, carried out in 2013 under the auspices of the United Nations (UN), is unavoidably political in its orientation. It states that while the peasantry historically has constituted a substantial proportion of the global population as a cognate group, it has been subject to political oppression; it has had to diversify into multiple forms of earning a livelihood; it concerns those who work, and often aspire to own, land belonging to others; and that peasant groups, inevitably, have dwindled as a proportion of the global population.[4] For his part, Leslie Mitchell was ambivalent about his peasant roots. In the lyrical Gibbon essay on 'The Land' in *Scottish Scene* the mature author reflects on his background with plangent nostalgia:

> I like to remember I am of peasant rearing and peasant stock. Good manners prevail on me not to insist on the fact over-much, not to boast in the company of those who come from manses and slums and castles and villas, the folk of the proletariat, the bigger

and lesser bourgeoisies. But I am again and again, as I hear them talk of their origins and beginnings and begetters, conscious of an over-weening pride that mine was thus and so, that the land was so closely and intimately mine (my mother used to hap me in a plaid in harvest-time and leave me in the lea of a stook while she harvested) that I feel of a strange and antique age in the company and converse of my adult peers [...]. (*Sm*83)

The two foundational tropes in Leslie Mitchell's personal mythology, one essentially philosophical and the other political, penetrated deep down into his rural roots. Mitchell's love of nature instilled in his formative years never left him. However, this was later tempered by an equally strong belief in agrarian socialism founded in concern for the poor farmers condemned to the effort to eke a living from such an unforgiving source. The author articulates his social sympathies most trenchantly in his 1931 novel *The Thirteenth Disciple*, in a passage deemed important enough for him to include it later in 'The Land' as a corrective to the common temptation to fall prey to rustic sentimentality:

> A grey, grey life. Dull and grey in its routine, Spring, Summer, Autumn, Winter, that life the Neolithic men brought from the south, supplanting Azilian hunger and hunting and light-hearted shiftlessness with servitude to seasons and soil and the tending to cattle. A beastly life. (*TD*10)

Mitchell identified wholeheartedly with the peasant, who came to represent for him the archetypal victim of political persecution. His radical socio-political convictions are based firmly on this heroically forlorn figure of the eternal underdog, a historical anachronism representing a throwback to a less sophisticated age in which fortitude was manifested chiefly as the stoical acceptance of the prevailing social order, in a world euphemistically shrugged off in Northeast vernacular as being 'illy parted'. Where the crofters of the Highlands of Scotland developed a collective solidarity that helped them to exercise a measure of control over the organisational reforms being enacted in farming society in the late nineteenth century, the crofters of the Northeast were much more politically acquiescent and therefore much more vulnerable to the demands of landlords and employers. James Mitchell's character reference from the factor overseeing his croft at Auchterless is a backhanded compliment to his self-defeating conservatism: 'he proved himself whilst there to be a capable and hard working farmer, thrifty and careful in all his dealings and thoroughly trustworthy'.[5]

Leslie Mitchell's background introduced him to the divided and divisive nature of Scottish rural society as a microcosm of the enduring inequalities persisting in Britain as a whole between the elite and the subaltern classes,[6] the sectors that in *Sunset Song* he designates simply 'gentry' and 'common' (*SS*51). From the circumstances of his own childhood Mitchell was made well aware of the social divide running throughout the rural Northeast; furthermore, where his father's generation was obsequiously accepting of its lot, Mitchell became ever more alert to the moral and political issues at stake and became ever more inclined to channel his dissatisfaction into concerted political action. With candid realism, unionised characters in the Epilude to *Sunset Song* are sardonically portrayed as mavericks paradoxically marginalised by their promulgation of communal doctrine espoused by the ploughmen's union and the farm servants' union (*SS*251). Traditionally, then, the Northeast is a rigidly hierarchical society marred by feudal divisions. Fundamentally patriarchal, historically it has also been vitiated by inflexible demarcation of gender roles – generally to the females' detriment; the whole issue of female rights was very much a taboo subject at this time. On the whole, Mitchell's righteous anger and his thirst for justice were rooted in his family life. Steadfastly, he was radicalised by his growing unhappiness with the manifest injustices of the society that he belonged to, to the point where finally he graduated to an uncompromising ideological stance in which egalitarian ends justified harsh revolutionary means. His father's first smallholding, the croft of Hillhead of Seggat in central Aberdeenshire, proved unworkable, forcing him to break his sixteen-year lease in 1907, not even halfway through his tenancy. When the Mitchells originally moved in at Whitsun in May of 1900, the whole venture was barely viable, due to the farm's exposed location and to its modest size, with only 45 acres of arable land. James Mitchell's plight was rendered even worse by the legal stricture obliging him to pay for materials required to improve the spartan farmhouse, which in turn triggered an increase of £1 in an already steep rent fixed at £36 per annum.⁷

The Mitchells fled to the bustling city of Aberdeen for a year on their escape from Auchterless, which rudely expanded the youngest son's social horizons, living in a heavily built-up area just off the main northern thoroughfare of King Street in the city centre and frequenting an urban school fully ten times the size of his first one back at Auchterless that he had attended for just two months. In May of 1908 the Mitchells moved south from the alien environment of the city to the croft of Bloomfield in the distinctive red clay land of the Mearns lying roughly midway between the cities of Aberdeen and Dundee, secured on a twelve-year lease. Eldest son George disappears from the record at this point before finally in 1920 emigrating to Canada, thereby depriving the croft of one of its most valuable assets. Yet again, though, the holding was not propitious: while the farm commanded a modest annual rental of only £15, it was only 37 acres in size (5 of which were accounted rough pasture), the farmhouse required substantial renovation and the location high up on the Reisk road, an area singled out in the Arbuthnott Estates' survey from 1919 as one that in agricultural terms was adjudged 'very poor indeed',⁸ contrasted sharply with the fertile parks gallingly spread out just a couple of miles below. (Young Leslie Mitchell's daily walk to school and particularly the uphill trudge home would have served as a constant reminder of the unfavourable appointment of the family homestead.) The modern-day fertility of the Mearns as a whole is largely attributable to the sweated labour of cultivation brought to bear by generations of farmers such as James Mitchell on heavy soil derived from underlying red sandstone that was dour and unyielding, and ineffably hard to work and to drain; the remarkable increase of 70 per cent in the acreage of tilled land specifically recorded in Kincardineshire in the nineteenth century is statistical testament to the fortitude of this rural workforce.⁹ To add insult to injury, James Mitchell's ability to make ends meet at Bloomfield was hindered from the outset by the debt that he was saddled with by his predecessor, summarily transferred to the new tenant within the terms of his lease with the estate.¹⁰

Leslie Mitchell's schooling and self-education proved his saving grace in a domestic environment where affection was muted, and in a community historically ranged against pretentiousness and pomposity in which his self-contained demeanour was construed as arrogance. His failure to marry his studies – principally his insatiable appetite for reading – with his daily regimen of farming chores prompted a commitment to finish his education at Mackie Academy in Stonehaven, the highest seat of learning for Kincardineshire. Following a thoroughly lukewarm beginning, Mitchell's senior school education came to a predictably unhappy end before completion of his first full session when the student walked out following an ungracious spat with one of the school's disciplinarian masters. Mitchell's valedictory award of second equal prizes in English and History and of Intermediate Certificates for Lower English and for Lower Drawing recorded in the subsequent summer prizes and merit lists made his ignominy complete. The departure from Mackie Academy represented an irrevocable break with formal education that subsequently was to haunt his whole adulthood.

Having narrowly avoided active participation in the fighting in the First World War by virtue of his youth (although he chanced his arm as a callow schoolboy in attempting to enlist in Aberdeen while he was underage), like countless other young men Mitchell spent the decade following the conflict drifting through all manner of menial jobs in a country that proved distinctly unwelcoming to its returning heroes. Initially, though, his abrupt departure from Mackie Academy was not as damaging as it might have proved as he quickly fixed up a highly congenial post as cub reporter with *The Aberdeen Daily Journal*, where he cut his teeth as a jobbing writer. The return to the scene of the Mitchells' urban hiatus proved providential. In his eighteen-month spell with the *Journal*, the more reactionary of the city's two major dailies whose circulation almost doubled in this period under the firm hand of legendary newspaperman William Maxwell, Mitchell gained a solid apprenticeship as a newshound at a time lurching towards the end of the war when the granite city, like the rest of Europe, was undergoing all sorts of acute social changes that gave rise to a slew of animated political responses.

Despite the ravages of the war, Leslie Mitchell indulged in the boisterous antics and high jinks commensurate with his age. As a young man, he was energised by the opportunities that the city offered by way of entertainment and edification; but the social deprivation that he was exposed to, especially on his reporter's round of the docks, advanced his political blooding markedly. The bittersweet Gibbon essay on 'Aberdeen' from 1934 reflects back on the social split dividing the city into the sedate middle-class areas such as Mannofield and Cults and the deprived areas such as the Gallowgate and Guestrow, with overcrowded streets in the city centre appearing long overdue for demolition. Fired up by political events abroad towards the end of the war, in Ireland, in Russia and in Germany, Mitchell tuned in to the political excitement brewing in his home city to the extent of attending political demonstrations led by prominent left-wingers such as John Paton, later Labour MP, and the irrepressible anarchocommunist Guy Aldred. Britain as a whole shared in the militancy born of this widespread sense of disenfranchisement and repression – and in Scotland feelings ran high among the working classes, whose pent-up frustrations harking back to social conditions existing from before the war spawned a multitude of radical political responses, most notoriously in Glasgow but also in Dundee, Fife and the central belt. Aberdeen also boasted a proud political reputation from the late nineteenth century onwards with strong socialist leanings particularly strongly in evidence at a grass-roots level, where the syndicalist Aberdeen Trades Council enjoyed close links with the three formal proletarian parties existing outwith the Labour mainstream across the UK – the Independent Labour Party (ILP), the Social Democratic Federation (SDF) and the British Socialist Party (BSP).[11] Mitchell's eighteen months in Aberdeen culminated in his clandestine election, as a reporter on duty, to the Aberdeen Soviet at a meeting of 'Bolshevist' sympathisers held at the Mealmarket Hall on Thursday 19 December 1918, a commendably early local response prefiguring the formation in Europe in 1919 of the Communist International, or Comintern, in keeping with the post-revolutionary aims of the left, of building internationally on the political gains won in Soviet Russia in 1917.[12]

Mitchell's move to Glasgow early in 1919 was a fillip for his self-esteem, as the promotion to the post of junior reporter on *The Scottish Farmer*, still Scotland's premier agricultural newspaper to this day, constituted tangible reward for the progress that he'd made in his apprenticeship at the *Journal*. The second city of empire was quite a step up from Aberdeen, however. Mitchell's digs were located in Garnethill, a vibrantly multiracial neighbourhood that was the traditional home to the city's Jewish and Asian communities far removed from the restricted racial demographic of the Northeast. More disquietingly, though, Glasgow exhibited social deprivation on a scale that was virtually unequalled in Europe, with industrial slums such as Camlachie, Govan and the Gorbals earning a shameful notoriety throughout the Western world. The political response from the nineteenth century onwards, resting chiefly on the cause of the miners, came to a head as Mitchell arrived in 'Red Clydeside' just as the legendary clash between protestors and the authorities known as Bloody Friday took place in George Square. The sheer extremity of the squalor and poverty that Mitchell witnessed subsequently in his five months in the city made an indelible impression on his social conscience; in his mature essay on 'Glasgow' in *Scottish Scene* the author is moved to declare, 'Glasgow, as no other place, moves me to a statement of faith' (*Sm*101), and his art is duly weaponised as a political sword dedicated to the cause of exposing and condemning the appalling conditions endured by the inhabitants of the slums:

> The hundred and fifty thousand eat and sleep and copulate and conceive and crawl into childhood in those waste jungles of stench and disease and hopelessness, sub-humans as definitely as the Morlocks of Wells – and without even the consolation of feeding on their oppressors' flesh. (*Sm*99)

At this time Mitchell was drawn into active political involvement with one of the welter of left-wing fringe groups that sprang into being before the formation of the CPGB in 1920, most probably Guy Aldred's Glasgow Communist Group, and his foolhardy embezzlement of his journalist's expenses, ostensibly on the party's behalf, resulted in his dismissal from the newspaper at a vulnerably tender age.

For the following ten years Mitchell suffered intermittent bouts of unemployment contingent with severe depression, promoting desperate recourse to the forces. He was a confirmed pacifist (who attempted in London in 1930 to form a pressure group called, with droll irony, the Society of Militant Pacifists), and yet he was forced to endure the demoralisation of a decade in military service just after the end of the war, having 'enlisted under the compulsion of hunger and unemployment', as he put it tersely in his first novel (*SR*13). Grubbing a living in the army was abject life-saving humiliation. After the war the allies pursued an increasingly aggressive political agenda within the unstable climate that had spread throughout the world, featuring the wholesale regrouping, reshaping and realignment of nations, with Britain assuming political control over Egypt and with Britain and France jointly benefiting from the division of spoils into so-called Mandates arranged under the aegis of the League of Nations from which Britain inherited Iraq, Palestine and Transjordan. In his four years in the Royal Army Service Corps (RASC), spread over two consecutive terms of enlistment flanking the demoralising climb-down of a return to the ranks, Mitchell witnessed the ruthless pursuit of draconian measures employed by the British in the Middle East concocted to reboot the spirit of empire by suppressing the forces of national insurrection, in Mesopotamia (Iraq), in Palestine and in Egypt.

His first term in the RASC featuring the chief posting to Baghdad was a baptism of fire that exposed him to the first wave of savage reprisals prosecuted by the British forces, involving torching of villages, mass executions by hanging and the blanket bombing of Arab outposts in order to vanquish the uprising now immortalised in Iraqi legend as the Revolution of 1920. Just as Britain's political power in Mesopotamia in the early decades of the twentieth century depended on the infamous Sykes–Picot Agreement, so the British presence in Palestine hinged on equally questionable legislation, the nefarious Balfour Declaration of 1917 (essentially fuelled by the Western distrust of Arab culture) that helped to destabilise the region and to escalate the conflict between the Arabs and the Jews by favouring the Zionist claims on the Holy Land, with the ultimate aim of creating a Jewish minority, British-controlled protectorate. Mitchell's second army enlistment began with a four-month posting to Jerusalem, where yet again he was privy to British tampering in the delicate affairs of the Middle East predicated on a strong military presence that reduced the country to a state of political and civic turmoil. Mitchell spent the bulk of his second attestation in the RASC, just over a year, stationed in Cairo, where yet again he arrived at a political hotspot. Egypt represented a deep-rooted historical legacy for the Western hegemony, with France and Britain steadily wresting the country from Ottoman control throughout the eighteenth and nineteenth centuries and the ruling Khedive in turn transformed into a vassal for British governance in direct defiance of the popular urge for national emancipation. Britain in fact had its firmest foothold in the Middle East in Egypt, having established its political influence there from the assumption of imperial control in 1882, secured in order to safeguard access to its colonies in Africa and Asia and, later, joint control with France of the Suez Canal. Following widespread nationalist protests after the war, it soon became clear that Britain couldn't maintain imperial rule in Egypt, and although Egyptian independence was nominally declared on 28 February 1922 – just three days after Mitchell's billeting in Cairo – the country endured uneasy relations with the covert British influence until its final severance in 1956.

While he avoided the industrialised slaughter of the trenches, then, Mitchell saw active service on the fringes of some of the most brutal military campaigns of the volatile post-war world. Technically, the RASC was a support regiment, but it was more of an auxiliary fighting force in that its soldiers served in active combat, most dramatically in Mitchell's case commanding a supply barge shuttling the fraught 280 mile journey south-east from Baghdad to Basra and back at a period when the indigenous hostility in Iraq ranged against the occupying British forces was at its zenith. Subsequently war came to embody for him one of the very worst maladies of civilisation and it recurs almost pathologically in his writing, most prominently in *The Thirteenth Disciple*, *Image and Superscription* and *Spartacus*. His first double term of military service at least offered the chance to travel throughout the Middle East, however, thereby providing valuable copy for narrative fiction. By contrast, his second spell in the forces, six years spent as a clerk in the RAF based in the south of England, gave him time and space to hone his writing skills, witnessing his first appearance in print in 1924 as well as the stabilising effect of his marriage in 1925 to Rebecca Middleton, his former neighbour and classmate from Arbuthnott. While latterly the RAF was mainly bankrolling

Mitchell's writing apprenticeship as he treaded water with his clerical duties (diffidently accepting promotion to Corporal), he also took part in political subversion in this period, especially during the toxic and divisive hostilities of the General Strike.

Shortly after their marriage Ray Mitchell suffered a life-threatening miscarriage acutely late on in her pregnancy, a trauma that served to strengthen the intimate bond existing between the couple. The lasting impact of Ray's near-fatality and the death of their new-born son can be traced in the theme recurring throughout Mitchell's fiction dramatising the dangers of childbirth, from the *Polychromata* stories 'Gift of the River' and 'Daybreak' to his novels *Stained Radiance*, picking over the pain of Ray Mitchell's eclampsia in harrowing detail, *The Thirteenth Disciple* and *Sunset Song* and *Cloud Howe*. The author's remarkable sympathy with the female lot and his subsequent engagement with gender politics were to a considerable extent stimulated by this excoriating personal ordeal.

Spurred on by publication in 1928 of his first full-length volume *Hanno: or The Future of Exploration* and by serialisation of his *Polychromata* stories in *The Cornhill Magazine* from 1929, Mitchell boldly struck out on his own and committed himself tirelessly from March 1930 to carving out a career as a full-time writer. The act of forsaking the security tendered by the armed forces in search of literary fame and fortune embodied a quite astonishing level of self-belief, especially given that the young couple once more were facing the imminent prospect of parenthood. At one point Mitchell even entertained the hazardous notion of self-publication, a scheme wisely abandoned as being ruinously expensive. More sensibly, along with the glut of aspiring writers seeking help in securing a precious source of income, he patronised several of the literary societies that had sprung up in response to the contemporary boom in public demand for reading matter of all kinds. His hard-won success within the London literary scene ultimately is testament to the generic qualities of stubbornness and singlemindedness that he inherited from his peasant ancestors, with the patronage of HG Wells and Leonard Huxley smoothing passage to the exclusive – indeed exclusionary – inner circle of literary society in the capital. Domestic contentment arrived with birth of a daughter, Rhea Sylvia, in 1930, followed by a son, Daryll, in 1934, and lured by the healthier environment existing outwith the city, from 1931 the Mitchells settled happily in the genteel London satellite town of Welwyn Garden City offering an agreeable enclave for a self-conscious counterculture formed by liberal-minded artists and professionals. The financial pressures relentlessly coming to bear on the practising author, however, were now palpable.

Throughout his last six years Mitchell went on to publish the astonishing total of sixteen full-length volumes of equally astonishing range, boasting fiction of all kinds and non-fiction on mainly historical subjects; the creative intensity was inspiringly productive but physically and emotionally draining. The appearance of Lewis Grassic Gibbon (the pen name adapted from his grandmother's name of Lilias Grassick [sic] Gibbon, passed down in slightly dilute form to his mother, Lilias Grant Gibbon) with the spectacular success of *Sunset Song* in 1932 cemented his reputation in Scotland and the United States in particular. In December 1934, faced with a gargantuan publishing schedule for both Mitchell and Gibbon titles, including an autobiography, a comparative study of world religions, a grandiose treatise on the history of humankind, a novel about William Wallace, a trilogy of novels concerning the Scottish Covenanters and a new Mearns novel featuring a female protagonist, Mitchell was laid low by an acute flare up of the chronic stomach ailment that had debilitated him periodically through adulthood. Eventually, on 4 February 1935, he underwent an emergency operation in Queen Victoria Hospital, Welwyn for a perforated gastric ulcer. On 7 February, a week before his thirty-fourth birthday, he died of peritonitis, a shockingly arbitrary and seemingly avoidable fate. Fittingly, following cremation in London, Leslie Mitchell's ashes were carried back by his widow to be laid to rest at Arbuthnott Kirkyard in the heart of the land that inspired his most enduring work. The central inscription on his gravestone, 'The kindness of friends, the warmth of toil, the peace of rest', taken by his widow from her husband's most famous book *Sunset Song*, poignantly summed up the homespun values that he himself lived by.

2

Narrative Preludes: *The Calends of Cairo* and *Persian Dawns, Egyptian Nights*

Leslie Mitchell belonged to the creative writing school subscribing to the belief that the discipline of constant practice was the key to success, and long before his work had earned publication he was constantly pestering friends and acquaintances for feedback on trial runs of his short stories. Having settled in Shepherd's Bush towards the end of his RAF service in the late 1920s, he went to enormous lengths to break into the productive literary world of London. He solicited the attention of high-profile writers and journalists, most successfully his boyhood hero HG Wells who supplied him with a testimonial used at the beginning of his first collection of stories *The Calends of Cairo* and who put him in touch with a literary agent as a practical help for him to place his early fiction work. In 1924 he had savoured the first taste of success with a story that scooped first prize in a competition run in *TP's and Cassell's Weekly*, one of the legion of popular newspapers that had sprung up to satisfy the popular demand for regular easy reading throughout Britain, a market that he patronised repeatedly thereafter as an outlet for his stories. Mitchell also attended amateur writers' gatherings in the city as well as undertaking a quest to cultivate useful contacts at soirées hosted by Wells, and he set out his stall accordingly to look the part of the young man of letters, augmenting the customary sartorial elegance of his professional wardrobe with optically redundant pince-nez, printed business cards, a personalised wax letter seal and photographic portraits taken on a regular basis for publicity purposes.

Mitchell's early published stories are apprentice work, clunky in conception and wooden in execution, and his use of the oriental lands that he'd encountered in the army constitutes a forced attempt to find an original voice, although his place setting appears convincingly authentic. The cultural impoverishment of the author's background followed by his prolonged detachment from the literary world during his extended travels in the army lend his early fiction writing a distinctly hackneyed air, from his *Polychromata* stories right through his first two autofictional novels and his imaginative romances. Mitchell's early literary models belonged firmly to the Victorian age, or at best to what is popularly known as the 'long nineteenth century' ending with the transformative cataclysm of the First World War. His literary heroes are largely forgotten nowadays, and their work had already begun to pall by the time he was an adult; consequently, they were of negligible value to his search for an original literary voice. In poetry – a surprisingly long-lasting creative urge on Mitchell's part – Ruskin, Morris, Swinburne and Edward Fitzgerald's English translation from 1859 of *The Rubáiyát of Omar Khayyám* have faded and slipped away to the margins of literary history, while his stylistic models for fiction, by Morris again, by John Galsworthy, Anatole France, Arnold Bennet and most of all by Wells, likewise provided a torpidly conventional context for his own artistic endeavours. With the advent of the war, the world was changed beyond recognition, and it took Mitchell several years to catch up with the corresponding changes in intellectual life, in art and in culture that had accompanied the highly charged socio-political climate. Nonetheless, while Mitchell's earliest stories can only really be accounted preludes to his mature fiction, the fraught relations developing in modern times between the West and the countries of the Middle East have given a new lease of life to these pieces beyond mere curiosity value.

Collectively, Mitchell's three series of Middle Eastern stories are a play on the genre of Arabian Fantasy – particularly the *Persian Dawns* sequence set in ancient Persia – fashioned in the West from traditional sources and developed in James Elroy Flecker's *The King of Alsander* (1914) and Joyce's *Ulysses* (1922) right up to the magical realism of Jorge Luis Borges in modern times. Mitchell took the form of the story-cycle from this formative source, but his fiction basically synthesises the romantic attractions of the mystical Arabesques associated principally with the *Tales of the Arabian Nights* with a more modern socio-political sensibility. 'Siva Plays the Game', his first published work, is much too archly plotted, and yet it gives a foretaste of some of the signature features of his imaginative writing. Pitting romantic and realist responses against each other, the story shows Mitchell's ambivalent attitude towards Egypt, towards the Middle East in general and indeed towards dilettante writers like his central protagonist who were crassly exploiting the inherent novelty and mysticism of the location in scabrous acts of cultural appropriation. While the twist ending simply underlines the enigmatic character of Egypt, though, there's a promising air of realism in the evocation of contemporary Cairo, with the old world colliding with the new as cars and donkeys jostle for road space, and with the opulent Continental Hotel in the European quarter hinting at the profound ethnic and cultural divisions of the region.

THE CALENDS OF CAIRO

The binary elements of realism and mysticism are rolled out fully in the *Polychromata* story-cycle that was published in Leonard Huxley's *Cornhill Magazine* each month from January 1929 onwards, featuring the welcome innovation of a first-person narrator, the White Russian dragoman, former Colonel Professor Anton Saloney who acts as urbane commentator on the action. Taken as a whole, these stories, later assembled in book form in *The Calends of Cairo* and continued in the *Egyptian Nights* section of the second collection, give a detailed impression of their distinctive setting. The title 'Polychromata' itself establishes the centrality of Mitchell's aim of creating a foundational spirit of place through his kaleidoscopic vision of Cairo, capturing 'the scents and smells of her, her days and nights, colours and chance voices' (*CC*92). The centrepiece of the stories is of course the River Nile and Mitchell shows a sound grasp of the greater geography of Egypt, including references to Alexandria and Giza as well as to the Sphinx and the Pyramids

– all popularised by Howard Carter's sensational archaeological discoveries in the early 1920s. The narrative is dotted with both archaic and exotic landmarks: Heliopolis, the plush European sector to the far north-east of the city, the Gamaijeh bazaar, the Khal Khalil (Khan al-Khalili, now known as the most famous market in the city), the Citadel with the Citadel Hospital, Bulaq Bridge. Already Mitchell's fascination with place is evident in throwaway descriptions, such as Saloney's vivid impression of 'that brown country, where stand in sleep the whitewashed villages under their smoke pencillings, and there is no other colour at all, but only the white and black' (CC87). Mitchell subtly introduces local colour by including a smattering of Arab words ('khatun', 'harim', 'pushi', 'bersim', 'jinui', 'haj', 'jihad') that, like his sparing use of Scots vocabulary later in the Grassic Gibbon fiction, adds to the flavour without detracting from the narrative flow; and he grounds his setting further with odd references to natural phenomena of the region, such as the Delta winds, the fly-riddled heat, the disease-carrying mosquitos, and to native Arab festivals, Muslim processions and devotional rituals like the drumming at Ramadan.

The characterisation in *The Calends of Cairo* reflects the polarisation of Cairo society symbolised in Mitchell's appropriation for the story 'East is West' of Kipling's imperialist mantra in 'The Ballad of East and West', affirming the permanent schism dividing the two cultures ('East is East, and West is West, and never the twain shall meet').[1] The story constitutes Mitchell's idealistic attempt in fiction to effect a comedic resolution to what are perceived by neo-imperialists to be insurmountable differences in race and culture. The bulk of Mitchell's characters in these stories are in fact migrants from Europe – from Russia, Germany, Greece, England and Scotland – as well as from America: some noble idealists, some idle tourists, some unscrupulous miscreants. The native population isn't individualised in the stories and remains a shadowy presence in thrall to the social circumscription of its locale, confined to the ancient streets and alleyways of Cairo's old city. However, contemporary political allusions infiltrate Mitchell's narrative, flagging up a series of measures adopted to combat the poverty and deprivation rife in the native quarters of the city. Jane Hatoun, plucky heroine of 'The Lost Prophetess' bent on winning female emancipation in Cairo by organising the Women's League of Al-Islam, is the fictional incarnation of the compelling struggle running throughout Egypt as a whole at the time of Mitchell's posting in Cairo moving towards a more enlightened form of Muslim belief embracing, among other things, an acknowledgement of female rights in the realm of education and in dress, the latter concerning the freedom to dispense with the wearing of the traditional veil, the pushi or burqa. Hatoun's chief adversary Shihada Bey is an accurate portrait of Muslim fundamentalism, a slick traditionalist and politicker who, despite his ingrained distrust of the 'English' who to all intents and purposes hold sway in Egypt, has wormed his way into favour with the ruling Khedive. Mitchell condemns Bey and all that he stands for through his caricature as a pantomime villain, offering as political antidote Ragheb Pasha, a liberal and outspoken critic of the most stultifying interpretations of Islamic dogma.[2]

Even Mitchell's earliest fiction writing has a reformist agenda, and the radical political temper of *The Calends of Cairo* can be gauged in passing references made to the German Spartacist Karl Liebknecht and to the Victorian reformers and founders of the arts and crafts movement John Ruskin and William Morris. Mitchell's early socialist utopianism is firmly embedded in the collection: in Jane Hatoun's martyrdom in the name of human goodness in 'The Lost Prophetess'; in the exalted studies of the selenologists in 'A Volcano in the Moon'; in Gillyflower Arnold's dream of fostering multilateral economic cooperation among nations in 'It is Written'; in Keith Landward's mission to create a workable world speech in 'Gift of the River'; in the moral admonishment of the antagonist's racist views enacted at the resolution of 'East is West'. At best, the Western influence is portrayed ambiguously. Most egregiously, in 'It is Written' the American mineralogist Gillyflower Arnold, employed by one of the nascent American oil companies in tandem with the Egyptian government to explore the desert in Bahaira (Beheira) in lower Egypt, demonstrates Mitchell's far-sightedness in recognising the quickening commercial scramble for oil, pleading gamely for international cooperation in the utilisation of this priceless finite resource.

PERSIAN DAWNS, EGYPTIAN NIGHTS

The *Egyptian Nights* stories, narrated by Sergei Lubow, a similarly engaging intermediary who is also a former teacher at the Gymnasium of Kazan, are even more upfront in dramatising Mitchell's understanding of the social and political complexities of contemporary Cairo. This second collection again moves easily around the city and its environs, with local colour adroitly added, in allusions to the cobbled streets, to the coldness of the winter nights. While Lubow milks the Cairo tourist season for personal gain, though, the Westernisation of the city is generally deemed to be unwelcome. The stories strenuously condemn the stark poverty that the indigenous population is consigned to within the overcrowded Warrens, and Mitchell specifically condemns the parasitical European influence in 'Dienekes' Dream' through the sardonic portrait of a representative *rentier,* a Parisian lawyer who has pitched up in Egypt to make a financial killing; indeed this story presents the most astringent denunciation of the economic straits that post-war Cairo has been plunged into, led by the Western rulers in what is branded a 'maelstrom of modernisation' (*PDEN*240). The force of opposition that emerges is fundamentally left-wing (the grass-roots socialist politics of the Cairene Labour Union wins a favourable mention in 'Revolt' [*PDEN*193]), but the revolutionary movement is tied most positively to the Egyptian Nationalist cause. The only viable political solution extended to the struggling Greek communards in 'Dienekes' Dream' comes from the sympathetic Nationalist lobby persisting among the ward masters and more actively from the students who are revolutionary Nationalists (*PDEN*236, 247). Most forceful of all, though, is Mitchell's portrait of the Egyptian realpolitik fashioned in 'Revolt'. This story dramatises the social interface prevailing in the early decades of the twentieth century between the native and non-native populations of Cairo, with Robert Sidgwick the English peddler of colonialist racism firmly opposed by Rejeb ibn Saud, leader of the ordinary people intent on fomenting a jihad dedicated to the aim of establishing 'the Green Republic of Islam' (*PDEN*188). Mitchell's naming of his Egyptian Nationalist visionary (the original title of 'One Man with a Dream', taken from Arthur O'Shaughnessy's popular Victorian 'Ode', being more indicative of the story's central theme) isn't coincidental: Ibn Saud, the famous Saudi potentate and statesman, rose in the inter-war period to become founder and king of Saudi Arabia. In addition, Rejeb ibn Saud's sophisticated background, including a European education, is reflective of the erudition of the real-life leaders of the Egyptian Wafd Party like Saad Zaghloul who were pivotal in the struggle towards the achievement of the country's independence between the wars. In the story, Sidgwick articulates the colonialist's complacent argument, deploring 'Nationalist extremists' and crudely denouncing 'this damn self-government foolishness' in the face of the unpalatable supremacist demand to 'treat a native as a native'. The intervention of his brother-in-law John Caldon voices Mitchell's own contempt for the sinister political situation that he found existing in Egypt at the time, admirably summed up as 'self-government – with an army of occupation' (*PDEN*184–5). The rejection by Ibn Saud of the chance to bring the insurrection to a violent head at the story's climax, thereby summarily terminating the people's fight to win social justice, shows Mitchell's own uncertainty over the rights and wrongs of revolutionary violence at the time, but this doesn't compromise his deep-rooted humanitarian principles insistently manifested here in a fictional Middle Eastern context.

The short 'Persian Dawns' story cycle is most notable for the author's ambitious extension of his narrative technique involving a collaboration between Nestorian bishop Neesan Nerses, author of an ancient thirteenth-century chronicle, and the translator who acts as interpreter for the contemporary reader. Notwithstanding the sensitivity of the 'apes as human' tale 'The Last Ogre', the formula, dependent upon romantic intrigue building up to opaquely unresolved endings, becomes laboured before the six constituent stories have played out, and while the sequence provides some insight to the world of ancient Persia, at this formative stage in his career the author now seemed to be running on empty within an ersatz fiction mode.

3

The Real Stuff of History: *Hanno, Niger, The Conquest of the Maya* and *Nine Against the Unknown*

One of Mitchell's pet haunts in London was the British Library with its iconic domed reading room, and as it had done with illustrious patrons such as Marx and Lenin as well as HG Wells, from his days in the RAF it afforded access within the one building to the whole gamut of source materials required for his own writing and research. Human rights dominated Mitchell's adult thinking, and he had an auxiliary fascination with human history that runs all the way through his four dedicated historical volumes, from his first slim published work *Hanno: or The Future of Exploration* from 1928 up through *Niger*, the Gibbon biography of his countryman Mungo Park, and *The Conquest of the Maya*, his most densely academic work, to his final published book *Nine Against the Unknown*, a rip-roaring biographical study of nine famous explorers tapping in to one of the memes from his childhood reading back at Arbuthnott School. It isn't hard to fathom where Leslie Mitchell's boyish excitement in the science and history of exploration came from, as an imaginative child brought up in a parochial cultural environment who was seeking intellectual escape from the physical confines of his home area.

The Conquest of the Maya includes two particularly illuminating passages that define Mitchell's self-image as a writer of history. The first, appearing out of context in the middle of the book, presents a strong case for legitimisation of the historian's prerogative to immerse his whole creative animus within his work, specifically promoting the subjective capacity of the imaginative writer to throw up radical new insight in both the selection of material and in the original manner of its presentation:

> The imaginative interpretation of puzzling, dazzling, or inexplicable personalities or epochs in history by poets and story-tellers is both legitimate and useful, as much for the light it throws on the psychology of the artist as for the fresh light his mendacity throws upon history. (CM133)

The use of the term 'mendacity' reflects the subversive purpose that Mitchell associates with his own particular brand of historical writing – linked with both his confirmed left-wing political standpoint and his Diffusionist beliefs with regard to human evolution. This viewpoint is developed in the second passage, more smoothly integrated within his narrative, which casts the true historian as an enlightened visionary who along with other iconoclasts is directly opposed to the entitled classes, and whose radical voice therefore is silenced:

> No doubt among the middle classes – the Guildsmen, the chilan priests – an individual might now and again arise who was *different* [italics in original text], who did or carved or said unconventional and unexpected things [...]. But of those imaginative, though not imaginary folk (for of them the real stuff of history is made), the records are dumb amidst the shouting of the captains and the kings. (CM217–8)

Mitchell's three major volumes of history measure up commendably to his aesthetic blueprint for the historian, as author of 'the real stuff of history', to act as eloquent legislator for the voiceless by combining empirical insight with narrative immediacy and a radical political sensibility. Where explicitly political fiction has always been viewed with some suspicion by the reading public – almost terminally so after the discrediting effect of the crudely standardised socialist realist programme reigning in the Stalinist era – theoretically at least, non-fiction writing has the apparent advantage of being anchored to actuality, an advantage that Mitchell sought to exploit.

Not only did Mitchell rate his historical studies on a par

with his fiction: he actually claimed first and foremost to be a historian – superficially a profession carrying a greater sense of gravitas. His approach as a historian was very much that of a political revisionist, intent on challenging received wisdom and righting wrongs traditionally done in expurgating or distorting the experiences of the past. In particular, he had been alerted in his background in Arbuthnott to the power wielded by the entitled classes through their monopoly of their powers of literacy and their ownership of documentary sources over long generations, to the detriment of the well-being of their social inferiors. This is one of the prime authorial motives driving *Sunset Song*, to redress the balance in favour of the disenfranchised echelons whose members' lives are excluded from the official annals and, as Robert Colquohoun affirms at the close of the book, to represent a sector of society for whom 'it was not in them to tell in words of the earth that moved and lived and abided' (*SS*260). Mitchell, just like Colquohoun, was the eloquent legislator for the subaltern classes, the Spartacus figure who in his writing was 'voice of the voiceless'. Subsequently, Mitchell maintains a strict polarisation between the rights of the subaltern classes and the elite, training the historical spotlight firmly on ordinary people – on the helot peasants of the ancient Mayan empires, on the refugees, slaves and poor tribespeople that Mungo Park encounters on his African adventures, on the Viking farmers of Leif Ericsson (also spelled Erikson, Eriksson and Eiriksson), on the natives of Guanahani encountered by Columbus in the Bahamas and on the simple Eskimo (Inuit) peoples who inspire Fridtjof Nansen's enlightened view of the world.

An equally sharp contrast distinguishing Mitchell's mature historical perspective is the stark distinction drawn between primitive and civilised societies. Fundamentally, this binary contrast represents the fulfilment of Mitchell's search for meaning amidst the post-war chaos where the carnage of the trenches had precipitated a wholesale crisis of faith. Mitchell was so highly attuned to signs of suffering and cruelty that he suffered regular nightmares about historical atrocities, and following the social misfortunes that dogged his tracks for the best part of a decade, he desperately yearned after a positive belief system to restore his faith in human goodness. His interest in the past stemmed from his boyhood, and his first essays from 1930 on Mesoamerica, a strangely arcane subject that held his attention throughout his professional career, are open-minded empirical products of thorough and systematic historical study. In the course of his researches Mitchell alighted on the Diffusionist interpretation of history, a quasi-political affirmation of the innate goodness of humankind in primal societies uncontaminated by civilisation that constituted a short-lived sideline in evolutionary theory during the first half of the twentieth century. The post-lapsarian phenomenon of civilisation is condemned wholesale as a freak accident attendant on the discovery of agriculture in the Nile Valley that led to the development and global dissemination of pretty much every malady of modern times: social stratification, organised religion, kings, gods, war. TS Eliot was one of the few fellow writers of eminence who also latched on to the ethical certainty held out by the theories of William J Perry, HJ Massingham and Grafton Elliot Smith as a potential gateway towards the forging of a true understanding of the past that thereafter had the potential to disclose possible means of creating a better future.[1] And indeed the conventional evolutionist Whig view of history advocating the steadfast progression of civilisation, as propounded most popularly by the British historian Herbert Butterfield in the early 1930s in direct opposition to the Diffusionist standpoint, didn't square at all easily with the wasteland vision of carnage and devastation lingering from the war.[2] Diffusionism cannot be accounted foundational in Mitchell's mature ideology, but it was of formative importance in securing a positive rationale for his thinking about humankind, in past, present and future. The profound moral and socio-political ramifications of Mitchell's adopted credo outweighed the tenuous historical principles on which it was founded, offering some prospect of relief from the all-pervading sense of ennui inherited from the war. Ultimately Diffusionism was both a blessing and a curse to the professional writer in stabilising his personal mythology while introducing a tendency towards glib tendentiousness in his more superficial works.

Throughout 1931 Mitchell raised his archaeological profile by publishing a raft of articles and reviews in respectable historical journals; subsequently his intensive study of the ancient

Mayan theocracies became increasingly sympathetic towards Diffusionist doctrine. By the summer of 1931 he had carved out a position as an expert on ancient American history with the respected journal *Antiquity*, publishing a study of the Incas and reviews of books on Peruvian history and Machu Picchu. 'The Diffusionist Heresy', his essay from the inaugural edition of *The Twentieth Century* in March 1931, a journal devoted to promulgating global disarmament, a cause célèbre of Mitchell's, gives a concise account of his gravitation towards Diffusionism and away from historical evolutionism. True to form, Mitchell embraced the most radical tenets of Diffusionist belief involving the blanket demonisation of civilisation as an aberrant and abhorrent development; his hagiographical portraits in *The Millgate Monthly* in 1931 and 1932 of two of the leading lights of the movement, Grafton Elliot Smith and William J Perry, proved his unswerving loyalty to its principles. While the historical researches of the Diffusionists are looked upon with a degree of scientific caution nowadays, their best works – Perry's *The Growth of Civilisation* (1924), HJ Massingham's *The Golden Age* (1927) and Elliot Smith's *Human History* (1930) – are invigorated by an enduring passion and an endearing idealism. Irrespective of the rather shaky historical foundations underpinning the Diffusionist theories, Mitchell found an anthropological prop for his belief in the human principles of freedom and equality enshrined in the politics of anarchism and communism. Even more importantly, his adherence to Diffusionism was essentially a moral impulse allowing him to maintain belief in his fellow men in spite of the scenes of unspeakable cruelty and violence that littered history from ancient times, and that constantly preyed on his mind.

HANNO: OR THE FUTURE OF EXPLORATION

As a first time author in his late twenties, Mitchell was desperate to parade his knowledge, and he crammed his erudition into *Hanno: or The Future of Exploration*, a sprightly speculative essay in the popular 'To-day and To-morrow' series reviving the form of 'the pamphlet' in which he let his imagination roam free for 10,000 words and indulged in winsome Wellsian fantasies about humankind exploring both distant space and the inner core of the earth. There's a touching worthiness to the study, with its gentle promotion of 'the sanities of universal co-operation' (*H*23), a fleeting anti-imperialist jibe at 'Europeanization' as 'synonymous with machine-gunning and concession-grabbing' (*H*38) and a timely condemnation of 'Signor Mussolini', with the threat of his expansionist foreign policy portending renewed political friction throughout Europe (*H*84). Most striking of all is the author's invocation of the need for 'the upbuilding of a workable Philosophy of Change' (*H*77), the first indicator of his mature fascination with a universal vision that came to meaningful fruition later in the supreme thematic achievements of *A Scots Quair*. Undeniably the volume's effectiveness as prophecy is compromised, with the reliability of the accurate predictions, of man's capacity to walk on the moon, to map the oceans and to develop the nuclear submarine, being offset by misjudgements such as his rubbishing of Einstein's theory of relativity and his questioning of Amundsen's capabilities as an explorer. Content-wise, then, the book is very much a period piece, but the vivid language use bodes well for the future imaginative writer, in his account of Hanno's historic voyage south and of the first moon landing, and even in throwaway passages such as the casual representation of the elevated perspective of contemporary American aviators, 'watching the mountain serrations below them, bare, snow-split, jagged, with the dun tundra swamps interspersing' (*H*31).

NIGER: THE LIFE OF MUNGO PARK

Diffusionist dogma makes a relatively understated appearance in *Niger*, Mitchell's revisionist study of his countryman Mungo Park, regarded together with David Livingstone as the leading light of the grand Scottish legacy of world exploration. The book's publication under the Gibbon pen name by The Porpoise Press, an Edinburgh publisher backed with the financial clout of Faber and Faber, signals the growing interest in Scottish affairs in Britain in the 1930s, but Mitchell himself never felt completely at home with the revival in national cultural awareness. *Niger*, though, is an impressive biography, with the author going back to the primary sources for his research, principally Park's own best-selling memoirs, and reconstructing his life and achievements with marvellous aplomb. In addition, the book is firmly placed in Scotland, historically, geographically and socially; it's immersed in traditional Scottish culture and beliefs; and its exploration of the ambivalences of the Scottish character and psyche rings resoundingly true. More subtly, *Niger* employs a polyphonic narrative voice that flits from the authority of the biographer's highly formal register to realistic dialogue and low-key mimicry of vernacular streams of consciousness. His final portrait was just too finely balanced for the Scottish establishment, however, and the disparaging reviews that he received at the hands of the Scottish press drew a typically stinging riposte by the beleaguered author in the form of a letter in which 'a Scots writer reviews his reviewers', knowingly attributing the backlash to extraneous factors to do with the peculiarly unforgiving nature of the Scottish sensibility embodied by intransigent contrarians who plainly 'kent his faither'.[3] The revisionist niche was wittily consolidated.

Viewed afresh, the Gibbon volume is in fact commendably objective in its assessment of the historical evidence. The early portion of the book delineating the rural childhood of the explorer spent in the Scottish Borders is a vicarious projection of the author's own upbringing, enthralled by the natural world all around him and yet subdued by the social and familial privations of his home environment. At the very beginning *Niger* gives a superb account of the quintessential Scottish peasant experience that produced quintessentially unique individuals such as Park – and Leslie Mitchell himself. The opening paragraph is vintage Mitchell, with the lushly portrayed scene of the rural Borders dissolving into a knowing reference to the peasant's remorseless workload that substantially blots out the sensuous charms elicited by such inspiring surroundings. The biographer is right there with his subject as a son starved of affection by stern god-fearing parents who viewed each other with what he knowingly dubs an 'iron tenderness' (N11), and even more so as someone sensitive to the stoicism expected of the female of the species – particularly in the child-bearing capacity of Park's mother, the uncomplaining progenitor of thirteen children. Subsequently Mitchell empathises readily with young Mungo Park on account of his isolation within his family. The equivalences with Leslie Mitchell's early life as son to a tenant farmer stack up as he's portrayed slogging miles on foot on his journey to school, being exposed there to vilification by his peers and stigmatised by his scholarliness, seeking solace in the natural world round about and inveterately finding escape in reading. Things are no happier at home, and the author writes poignantly of the son's unfulfilled craving for a father's affection snatched occasionally at night-time in 'the touch of a rough-grained hand on his cheek' (N12). This gives rise to a heartfelt denunciation of the plight of siblings born within a family whose ingrained ethos is so severely pragmatic, vividly presented by the author with satirical recourse to lightly focalised vernacular:

> But that [paternal signs of affection] unseldom, for it would have been gypèd foolishness, and folk must work, and get on with their work, and see to the making of silver, and that all the bairns are well-rigged when they gang to the kirk of a Sabbath. Of unnecessary affection, none. (N13)

Park proceeds to suffer the loneliness that Leslie Mitchell's own academic prowess found for him at Arbuthnott School and at home at Bloomfield, and even the latent arrogance encapsulated in the popular anecdote of Mungo's laddish pledge to become a famous man of letters is diminished by the author's reporting of his mother's withering retort, a 'national' reflex again echoing his own parents' impatient dismissal of his literary aims:

> 'You poor useless thing, do you think that you will ever write books?' (N15)

The victim's sense of alienation and his withdrawal into himself and his retreat to the world of nature are all keenly felt by Mitchell as he concludes knowingly:

> Books, and still the solitudes of the hills and windings of Yarrow, remained to comfort him from both the raucous voices of his schoolmates and the fatuous expectations of Fowlshiels. (N16)

The desire of Park's parents for their gifted son to channel his academic abilities into the pursuit of the most highly coveted

Presbyterian career aspiration of a religious calling sparks off a typically incisive disquisition on the banal pragmatism of the Scots affinity for the ministry. Mungo's refusal to comply with their wishes therefore counts heavily in his favour, and Mitchell, already famous as author in *Sunset Song* of one of the foremost works of ecofiction, indulges in a nostalgic backwards glance, casting the rejected Park in his own image, in the image of Chris Guthrie, of young Ewan Tavendale, independent and alive to the natural world:

> Mungo had lain on the grass and the heath and the bells of the hills, looked at the twining convolutions of the buttercups, the purple bells of the heather-drops, watched the busy insect-world at its play of life, looked at the blood pulse down the veins in his own arm. He had seen the play and perhaps the majesty of life. (N18–19)

The sense of kinship conjured in the opening chapters between author and subject is effectively severed from chapter three onwards, but Leslie Mitchell's early exposure to the racial diversity of the Middle East also equipped him experientially for the task of making sense of the bewildering ethnological complexities that his subject encountered on his travels in fin-de-siècle Africa, a war-torn continent riven by racial power struggles and in which fractious tribalism was very much the norm. While Mitchell could readily empathise with Park's formative background, however, he's notably less sympathetic in his representation of the ends that Park channelled his extraordinary personal qualities towards in adulthood. Mitchell brings out the explorer's twin-edged accomplishment, devoting two-thirds of the text to tracing the fortitude of Park's first, two-year-long, expedition to locate the River Niger against the manic desperation of the second attempt to find its mouth revealing Park's hubristic misjudgement that caused so many deaths – including his own. Mitchell's moral judgements are now significantly harsher: he condemns Mungo's piousness as a hypocritical motivation behind his exploits, viewed as manifestations of odious British colonialist enterprise; he subjects Park's own written accounts of his adventures to critical scrutiny, frequently questioning their veracity; he denounces Park for going along with the prevailing Western stance adopted in tolerance of slavery; and, most compelling of all, he teases out the curious psychological profile of a fellow Scot whose social and cultural background proved the testing ground for feats of almost unparalleled fortitude, ultimately paving the way for flaws of judgement of equal magnitude and even greater consequence.

Beyond its categorisation as biography, the Gibbon portrait of Mungo Park is a compelling mapping of relentlessly misdirected ambition following the classic determinist tradition in Scottish fiction centring on protagonists of self-destructive megalomania – Robert Louis Stevenson's *The Strange Case of Dr Jekyll and Mr Hyde* (1886), George Douglas Brown's *The House with the Green Shutters* (1901), J MacDougall Hay's *Gillespie* (1914), AJ Cronin's *Hatter's Castle* (1931). Despite its erudition, its narrative sweep and its psychological understanding, the author's fears that his biography would prove too challenging for the Scottish establishment were made manifest in the critical neglect that the book has suffered from first publication.

THE CONQUEST OF THE MAYA

The Conquest of the Maya is Mitchell's most sustained academic work, appropriately dedicated to his old headmaster Alexander Gray. His historical approach combines his academic nous and narrative skills in a convincingly argued account, intended to rival WH Prescott's massively popular *History of the Conquest of Mexico*, of the strange efflorescence and even stranger disappearance of one of the world's grandest civilisations. Clearly he relished the intellectual challenge posed by the Maya, with their advanced art and architecture and unique writing and calendrical systems, whose influence extended all the way through the southern Mexican states, the Yucatán Peninsula and the northern Central American region from 2000BCE, reaching its peak from 200 to 900AD and surviving right up to the arrival of the Spanish conquistadors in the sixteenth century. Impressive as his research is, however, most successfully deployed in the passages dealing with the architecture, art and history of the Mayan Old Empire and in his profile of the more recent history of the Mayan New Empire in Yucatán, Mitchell pursues a narrow line of argument bending the facts to promote the Diffusionist point of view.

Archaeological research carried out since Mitchell's lifetime has largely contradicted the heliocentric thesis of Diffusionism, with the earliest European civilisations being found to precede the origins of Egyptian civilisation and with evidence of specific indigenous societies coming to light across the globe whose subsequent evolution was free of outside influence.[4] With regard to Mesoamerica, Mitchell argues that the trappings of civilisation arrived from Egypt with successive waves of immigrants bringing their own rituals and cultures, the author identifying Egyptian-style iconography in early Mayan monuments and taking pains to argue that fundamental Hindu influences can be found scattered throughout the Mayan and Mexican regions. The importance of the Diffusionist world picture is fully, if mechanically, expounded in the second chapter of the book focusing on the prehistory of America before the Maya.

Mitchell customarily approached human history in terms of its torments and tribulations rather than its triumphs, and within a society revolving around institutionalised barbarism, ritualistic sacrifice, hierarchical privilege and religious perversion his sympathies come to rest on the ordinary citizens who fall prey to the cruelty of rulers and priests. In chapter five, 'Life in a City of the Ancient Maya', the author gives free rein to his imaginative powers in order to reconstruct everyday life in the pre-Columbian theocracies as experienced by ordinary folk. His subaltern loyalties are once again to the fore in his concentration on the people's sufferings and come to rest on the empathy that he shows with the natives who till the land, who evince 'the immemorial attitude and plod of the peasant' (*CM*153) and on whose labours in fact the whole society depends, as he declares flatly, 'Maya existence was built on the lives and work of the helot peasantry' (*CM*189). Mitchell returns to their plight all the way through the book, personally identifying with the primitive nature of their agricultural tasks, with their rude smallholdings, with their sardonic disdain for their masters, with their self-defeating stoicism in the face of the Spanish invasion. Just as in *Sunset Song*, he tunes in to the exasperating ambivalences of their character, mixing a dour fortitude with an intractable reluctance to translate their time-worn grievances into political action – one of the key tensions pervading his political outlook. The conclusion of the book wryly extends a measure of comfort, however; just as the Kinraddie and Mowat dynasties in the trilogy come to an ignoble end, suffering the fate common to all humanity, so the elaborate achievements of the Mayan civilisation, shrouded in thick jungle and lost in the mists of time, are finally put into ironic perspective in the closing paragraph of the Epilogue that sums them up as 'a little people, a little cult, dreaming its dreams and passing' (*CM*269).

NINE AGAINST THE UNKNOWN: A RECORD OF GEOGRAPHICAL EXPLORATION

As Mitchell's last published book, it's not surprising that *Nine Against the Unknown* should exhibit a flowering of the author's ideas and beliefs. At first glance, the volume seems to be a fairly conventional romp through eminent feats in world exploration in the second millennium after Christ, from the primitive heroism of Leif Ericsson's adventurings in about 1000AD through the intrepid exploits of Marco Polo, Christopher Columbus, Cabeza de Vaca, Magellan, Vitus Bering, Mungo Park and Richard Burton up to Fridtjof Nansen's more fully documented contemporary achievements. Individually, the portraits are action packed and surprisingly detailed, representing a multitude of races, religions, societies, customs, beliefs. The historical backdrop unfolds a coherent vision of global history, of outstanding individual enterprise fuelled by, and fuelling, national exceptionalism and rapacious jingoism in which the stock Diffusionist condemnation of civilisation graduates into an anti-colonial denunciation of imperialist greed throughout the centuries. The majority of the monographs – indeed all apart from the portraits of de Vaca, Bering and Nansen – emulate *Niger* in their ironic take on the highly acclaimed ambitions of their subjects, building up a convincing picture of misguided endeavour and, ultimately, of human futility.

The final study of the Norwegian explorer-turned-politician Fridtjof Nansen brings the volume to an affirmative conclusion, however, as Mitchell finds in his biography the model of a life lived to the full and signifying a practical commitment to exalted principles – ethical, environmental, political and philosophical. Nansen is represented as a truly inspiring figure: an eminent explorer whose life, shaped by his sensitivity to the natural world, was channelled into political activism carried out under the auspices of the League of Nations, which Mitchell the self-proclaimed cosmopolite hails as 'the conquest of pity and compassion, perhaps the truest conquest of all' (NAU316). More profoundly, Mitchell's bracing depiction of Nansen's neo-Romantic epiphany experienced in the Arctic wastes of Greenland captures the fundamental isolation of humanity, the existential legacy that's the human birthright. Like Chris Guthrie, his real-life paragon is at one with nature. Mitchell's final hero is both intimidated and exhilarated by the near-spiritual understanding that finally he receives of the physical majesty of his surroundings and that subsequently engenders a selfless humility that galvanises him into dedicating his life towards improving the human lot:

> He would walk out on the ice alone and stand and look at that great arching of the Galaxy above him and realize again the loneliness of man, what a little adventure in truth was his, how strange the puny aims and hopes and fears he had in this brief flicker of light betwixt darkness that he called life. (NAU309)

The author advocates an ardent cosmopolitanism throughout his most mature writings, most passionately in the final portrait that he paints here of Nansen, a prime motivator behind the League of Nations. Yet this final book is more profoundly pertinent. Mitchell's ideology places him in a post-Romantic/pre-Absurdist limbo where the restriction to an atheist view of the world proves a liberation in facilitating the pursuit of secular creeds capable of improving our transient lives. Mitchell takes his grand philosophical vision a stage further in *Nine Against the Unknown*, as he does also in the fiction of *A Scots Quair*, where the clinical materialism of the post-war era is softened by his environmental convictions, specifically his belief in the natural universal process of everlasting change, into a basically pagan acceptance of the organic life-force endlessly being reworked in the process of birth, life and death – the philosophical bedrock of his own rustic legacy.

4

Autofiction: *Stained Radiance* and *The Thirteenth Disciple*

As is often the case with early novels, Mitchell's are best classed as autofiction in that they deploy the medium of imaginative literature for interrogation of his own past fundamentally in search of some kind of salutary perspective on his life.[1] The first two novels are especially important in shedding light on his background (and on his considered retrospective response to it), although they deal with events in reverse chronological order: *Stained Radiance* explores the immediate past of his time in London in between the wars and in the RAF, while *The Thirteenth Disciple* delves back further to his boyhood in rural Aberdeenshire – home, school, family life, employment in journalism in Glasgow and his political indoctrination.

STAINED RADIANCE: A FICTIONIST'S PRELUDE

Published at last in September 1930 and aptly dedicated to his wife whose staunch support of her husband had actually included collaborating on the editing of his first novel, *Stained Radiance* bears the scars of its prolonged period of gestation and of endless revisions: the final text is overcomplicated, overwritten and freighted with self-conscious literary quotation and discourse on art and literature, politics and philosophy. Complete with its brazenly lascivious art deco dust jacket ('why on earth a rather well executed picture of two nude, normal and rather good-looking human beings should shock the reading public is a problem that might stagger even Dr. Freud', Mitchell quipped disingenuously to Alexander Gray[2]), the book was clearly pitched at a select middlebrow readership. In the final analysis, however, it's a fascinating record at a fictional remove of the author's experiences as a young adult, of his radical political development and of the evolution of his innermost thoughts about contemporary society. The novel's social setting proffers an unforgiving picture of the early twentieth-century world at peace and at war as a damning state of the nation critique, and the interrelated storylines of the twin protagonists John Garland and James Storman finally snuff out all hope of ordinary people finding concrete ways forward; the dead-end represented in the stagey exchange of roles manufactured at the end of the book destroys any substantive hopes for the future that the reader may have harboured. Admittedly at the book's resolution Garland rediscovers a sense of political mission and, more poignantly, Storman invests his future hopes in his infant son, reflecting the optimism that the author himself felt at the time of writing at the prospect of becoming a father. The overarching bleakness of the novel, though, alternating abrasively between gritty social realism and ironic nihilism, undeniably captured the spirit of the time, with the radiance of the title (lifted from Shelley's 'Adonais') all but extinguished by the all-pervading stain; but in purely commercial terms – now the jobbing author's uppermost concern – the book was destined to undersell.

In *Stained Radiance* the reader identifies most with Garland and with his lover Thea Mayven, a prototype of Chris Guthrie. Mitchell draws on his RAF service for Garland's characterisation, but Thea is the most heavily autobiographical figure, sharing his love–hate relationship with his rural roots. She is introduced in terms of conflicting emotions – 'Scots, she had never ceased to feel foreign in London, and intrigued by it' (*SR*2) – but her love of the countryside articulating 'the sad romantic realism of the peasant' (*SR*3) produces the most lyrical passages in the book. Her skittishness about her 'heritage of the earth' (*SR*3) poignantly captures the author's own inner turmoil; nonetheless, the Scottish passages in both the opening novels appear quite comforting, like Mitchell's annual family holidays back in the Mearns and in Aberdeenshire offering homespun relief from the frenzy of the city. Thea clearly possesses Chris Guthrie's spirit of independence, delicately shown in the passage describing her open physical self-appraisal (*SR*51), and her intimate 'Odyssey' tracing her developing consciousness as an individual foreshadows Chris's questing intellect (*SR*82) while discreetly paralleling James Joyce's modernist citation of classical myth. Mitchell tries out a few alternative approaches concerning the deployment of Scots language, from the conventional jarring dichotomy of yoking together formal English narrative and colloquial Scots dialogue, to integrating interior monologue within the third-person narrative, and dispensing with intrusive inverted commas normally used for speech. Thea again is the one who is given to reflect on the lasting place of 'the good Scots' as the appropriate medium for painting traditional rural experience, in a passage looking forward to Long Rob's stout defence of his native tongue at Chris's wedding:

> She found herself remembering long-forgotten words of the good Scots, canty, lightsome words and jingles, things with old laughter and the smell of the peats and sea in them; darksome old words like clanjamfried and glaur and greep, words wrought for the bitter winter nights by the plodding peasants of the Eastern seacoast … . (*SR*162)

The Garlands directly represent the troubles that the Mitchells had suffered in their early married life in London, in a city racked by profound housing and employment problems. Garland's despondence at what he terms 'the rottenness called Life' (*SR*117) is shared by Storman, whose disillusionment is expressed in a more specific denunciation of 'the cold-blooded inhumanity of man' (*SR*145). Indeed in his preliminary incarnation as hard-bitten political agitator and secretary of the Anarchocommunist Party Storman foreshadows staunch CP man Jim Trease and young Ewan Tavendale in *Grey Granite*, despite the climactic crisis of faith that leads him to defect. Garland's final affirmation of 'the unknown beauty of London' (*SR*206) shows Mitchell's familiarity with the city's geography although overall the urban setting only adds to the unforgiving tone of the novel, reflecting the hopelessness of the mass of ordinary people abandoned in its streets after the war.

Mitchell presents the reader with a full-on portrayal of the social iniquities of inner London, and while this situation is seen to foment a proliferation of left-wing political responses, no single ideology emerges that offers any real promise of improving matters. Mitchell's own stock revolutionary icons are invoked throughout the novel, from Spartacus to his characteristically politicised figure of Christ, to Buddha, Marx and Lenin, and snatches of lyrics from the principal left-wing anthems of 'The Internationale' and 'The Red Flag' are transcribed in the text. Through the intertwined lives of Garland, Storman and Andreas van Koupa (the latter two steadily declining into lapsed revolutionaries), however, Mitchell questions the general efficacy of the radical political parties charged with improving the common lot.

Storman's commentary on the political scene in Britain in the 1920s in the opening chapter directly represents the author's own jaundiced viewpoint as he analyses the devastating impact of the failure of the General Strike in May 1926 upon all left-wing parties, in particular with regard to the comprehensive popular disillusionment with the Labour Party that had refused to endorse the action. Satirical set pieces directly looking forward to the political caricature of *Cloud Howe* and *Grey Granite* lampoon the various political parties of the time, from the annual congress of the Anarchocommunist Party in chapter four that degenerates into egotistical mudslinging to the by-election in chapter seven that serves up risible caricatures of the mainstream parties' candidates – including, prophetically, fascist blackshirts bolstering the Conservative campaign. This steady stream of political irony culminates in Storman's insipid address of the South Wales Anarchocommunist Party that highlights the anaemic nature of local working-class agitation as the members grasp at empty slogans and clichés and regurgitate hollow political rhetoric.

Mitchell was constantly reflecting on the purpose of literature, and his fiction has a strong subtext running through it focusing on writers and their work. As he does so often in his fiction, in *Stained Radiance* he plants metafictional clues within his narrative that hint at his own literary aims. John Garland, in many ways a mirror image of the author himself as airman, practising communist, rationalist and aspiring first-time novelist, sets out his stall early on in the novel when he reflects on the 'lack of purpose' among contemporary novelists (*SR*58–9). An even more critical commentary on contemporary literature is embodied by the satirical subplot featuring the lairy figure of Andreas van Koupa, who sells out to author preciously esoteric works whose primary motivation becomes quite transparently mercenary and self-interested. Mitchell's final comment on the moribund state of literature at the time is summed up in the novel's closing subchapter, in which Koupa sets all his former agonising about life and about his creative vocation aside and surrenders all artistic credibility in the pursuit of hedonistic gratification with his submissive patroness-consort.

THE THIRTEENTH DISCIPLE: BEING PORTRAIT AND SAGA OF MALCOM MAUDSLAY IN HIS ADVENTURE THROUGH THE DARK CORRIDOR

Mitchell bowed to his publisher's advice by grafting a happy ending on to *The Thirteenth Disciple* (and later to *Image and Superscription*), and yet the spurious leap of faith contrived at the book's close is stymied and effaced by the deeply entrenched sense of despair built up in the evocation of the existential 'dark corridor' in the preceding chapters. The arresting title of *The Thirteenth Disciple* isn't explained, but the declarative self-affirmation associated with the last of Christ's apostles who replaced Judas obliquely captures the author's own self-image as a latter-day iconoclast. The book itself is an incongruous conflation of social realism and 'lost world' fantasy, with a Diffusionist message crudely integrated within a narrative that, as Mitchell himself disclosed in the coda added to the synopsis of his autobiography, draws liberally upon the raw matter of the author's early life.[3] Formally released in January 1931, *The Thirteenth Disciple* was the only Mitchell novel published that year, a marginally more upbeat tale of protagonist Malcom Maudslay's search for truth in the post-war world with easily recognisable autofictional elements stretching back to his upbringing in the Northeast. The early chapters chronicle the author's own shaping by the farming communities that he was raised in, reworking his education at Arbuthnott Parish School and his subsequent removal to journalism and left-wing politics in Glasgow, with a curiously discordant genre-bending jump into the jungle of Central America in search of 'the City of the Sun itself' (*TD*252) pasted on melodramatically at the book's end. The archetypally difficult second novel inevitably hadn't quite the dramatic impact of his first but it also exerts its own fascination, in its bracing autofictional elements, in its forthright confrontation of urgent socio-political themes and in its authentic Scottish interludes drilling deep down into his roots. The outwardly idealistic gloss at the climax, revolving around the protagonist's dying fulfilment of his archaeological quest in Central America and the posthumous birth of his son back in England, looks ahead to the more palatable and marketable idealism of his imaginative romances.

Mitchell can now be seen freely experimenting with narrative technique, creating a layered intertextuality set out in the prefatory 'A Footnote on Origins' defining the varied literary sources of his narrative: his protagonist's abandoned autobiography, his diary, portion of an autobiographical novel and a privately published book of Malcom's verse, all supplemented by eyewitness testimony and transcribed interviews. These representational modes add a welcome sense of variety; as yet, however, Mitchell lacks the sophistication (and confidence) to steer his reader through the kind of innovative narrative boasting the fragmented unreliability of Grassic Gibbon's protean voice. In addition, the storyline tracing the romantic fortunes of Malcom Maudslay, first with Rita Johnson and then with Domina Riddoch, is undeniably gauche, and on the whole the author's characterisation beyond the febrile contradictions of his autobiographical persona is disappointingly one dimensional. However, Mitchell's interest in strong female protagonists, 'New Women' who are political emblems commanding their own destiny in personal, social, economic and sexual terms, may be seen to carry over from *Stained Radiance* with moderate success. Like Thea Mayven before, Domina is a liberated figure who personifies the sexual *mores* of the 1920s – and while her figure also lacks roundness and depth, she attains symbolic status early in Book Two where she gives vent to the pent-up historical rage of the proto-feminist 'crusader', resolving:

> '[…] all those poor damn women who went through hell to give the dirty peasants and priests and patriots and poets of civilization easy times and well-cooked food and all the crazy satisfactions of

lust and torture and sadism which were yours – I'm going to live every unenjoyed life of those starved mothers of mine who were killed and eaten in cannibal rituals, starved to death, beaten to death, crippled in crinolines and ghastly codes, robbed of fun and sunshine and the glory of being fools and disreputable for over six thousand years ... . And I'm going to get every woman alive to do the same!' (*TD*179)

Mitchell's hardening politics are represented in the humorous study of the Secular Control Group, a bourgeois gathering of well-intentioned dreamers idly attempting to transform their post-war angst into a cohesive plan of campaign. Their eleven-point political agenda constitutes a wish-list of serious-minded social solutions, and the three wilfully challenging principles advocating sexual equality by vouchsafing social, biological and economic rights are placed first in the list of 'social and political' aims by the wilfully challenging author:

(i) Abolition of the Legal Status of Marriage.
(ii) State Propaganda and Enforcement of Birth Control.
(iii) A General Tax to be levied for the Endowment of Each Woman's First Two Children. (*TD*215)

The more fully extended Scottish-set sections appearing in the first four chapters of the book are most memorable overall, faithfully recreating the author's own upbringing and his radical political shaping. The naturalistic observation of people, places and actions looks forward directly to the trilogy, and Malcom's love–hate relationship with the farm prefigures Chris Guthrie's internal conflict, on the one hand denouncing its 'grey, grey life' and on the other savouring 'memories of those early days in Leekan of which he never wearied' (*TD*10). The account of Malcom's education in Leekan Parish School and of his own astounding reading programme draws a wry acknowledgement of the nerdishness that worried his own mother, 'lest his brain should soften', and that made him 'a consummate failure as a farm-labourer' (*TD*24–5). The succeeding watershed in Malcom's life, just like the author's, deals with his dawning interest in socialism as his abrupt departure from further education leads Malcom to journalism in Glasgow, where his social sympathies are hardened by the prevalent signs of poverty and squalor. Malcom's gravitation towards the radical Left Communist Group appears an entirely logical development.

Prophetically, the author expressed misgivings about the perils of drawing directly on his background in the Northeast, writing to Alexander Gray:

> The particular locality has such a close resemblance to Arbuthnott and the Howe o' the Mearns generally that I was forced to insert a few entirely fictitious topographical details – in case some enraged Reisker or other fauna sued me for libel.[4]

As Mitchell was to find just eighteen months later with the tetchy local reception reserved for *Sunset Song* back home in the Mearns, verisimilitude of such immediacy could be adjudged to be just too near the bone.

Towards the end of Book One Mitchell wanders away from his own life experience, although the disturbing account of Malcom's failed suicide had some basis in the author's own desperate reaction to his sacking from *The Scottish Farmer*. The representation of the horrors of the war in the trenches at the Somme is still unsparingly graphic, however, and the transposition of Malcom's mild-mannered brother Robert into the cauldron of death and destruction acts as the final indictment – just like Ewan's sense of alienation in military service at the climax of *Sunset Song*. Mitchell had done his homework well, plunging his protagonist into the bloodiest battles that historically took place in Northern France, at Delville Wood, Trônes Wood, Longueval and Ginchy; his subsequent portrayal of Malcom's post-war convalescence and rehabilitation in central London in late 1923 and early 1924 poignantly refers back to Mitchell's own catastrophic slump in fortune suffered at that exact time. The therapeutic return to Leekan is represented in suitably sensuous terms that hark back with affection to Mitchell's own default homing instinct to seek out the solace of the Mearns countryside in the wake of his worst travails.

Mitchell is incisively frank in his portrayal of the catastrophic loss of faith that Malcom observes all around him in post-war Britain and that he experiences himself as he enters the godless era, and 'secured books by Huxley and Haeckel and rejoiced with them at the discomfiture of the Deity' (*TD*23). Anatole France, author of one of the novel's principal epigrams, is again cited in Malcom's reading, while the philosophical scepticism of the age is best captured in a typical reductive metaphor in which Malcom is shown to conceive of military life as the workings of a giant ant-hill (*TD*104), and the fragility of human life as a whole is apprehended later in the same chapter with bald materialist pragmatism as 'only a temporary grouping of atoms endowed with a conceit called personality' (*TD*115). To compound matters, the urgency of the social problems caused by rampant industrialisation, by economic disintegration, later by the war, promotes mass left-wing political activity, the resultant failure of socialist politics being succinctly summed up in Malcom's alarmist term as 'the collapse of the entire socialist philosophy' (*TD*66).

Meierkhold's political disillusionment reinforces the overweening sense of spiritual despair. Subsequently shaken by his own personal traumas, by the loss of his wife and unborn child and by his enforced mercy killing of his best friend Metaxa at the Somme, Malcom articulates the perennial questioning of religious belief that the carnage of the First World War throws up even now, asking, 'God, what thinking can answer that, what God or faith justify that horror?' (*TD*166). Further disillusionment follows with the failure of the General Strike, the fallout from which threw the British left-wing rank and file into corrosive disarray, which Mitchell rightly uses in turn to criticise the mainstream political parties charged with attending to the welfare of the people at this crucial juncture in the rehabilitation of the country and of the world at large.

Mitchell thought long and hard about the ends of his artistic endeavours, and his second novel makes two particularly telling references to this theme. The dawn of a new era, godless and faithless, symbolically welcomed by the local bonfire ushering in the new year, is seen to demand a new artistic response as Malcom perceives that the conflagration 'flamed on a gaseous literature and an idiot art' (*TD*12). At this point the author's deep-rooted literary sardonicism is inextricably bound up with his overweening scepticism in relation to the world in general. The more specific application of the author's unhappiness with literature to that of Scottish provenance hints at the much more productive response of Grassic Gibbon fashioned less than two years later; the impatience that Malcom shows with sanitised Scottish fiction constituting 'romantic novels of claymores and stag-hunting and bonnie brier bushes' (*TD*6) is the first sign of the deep-seated disgruntlement with stock representations of Scottish national identity that underpinned Mitchell's greatest creative achievement.

Although the author's diagnosis of the ills of post-war society is invigoratingly honest, his prescribed remedy is unconvincing. Chapter two presents a formulaic Diffusionist homily as Malcom condemns 'the base shames and tabus of civilization that befoul the clean desires of the healthy human animal' (*TD*32). Subsequently Domina and Metaxa indoctrinate Malcom into the teachings of Diffusionism, which promotes a reasonably clear clarion call in a non-conformist attack on 'the old, cobwebby religions, and the old and useless political parties' (*TD*208–9). Sadly, though, the new dogma isn't given any practical substance, and Mitchell's imaginative wish-fulfilment at the book's climax, of Malcom's intrepid expedition in search of the legendary lost city of the Maya that sustains a valedictory vision of 'the City of the Sun itself' just before his death, stranded all alone in a remote cave in Central America, brings the book to a bathetic close that's no more convincing for the lyrical natural imagery used to gild the hero's dying vision (*TD*252–3).

In the final analysis, *The Thirteenth Disciple* raises profound questions about life-changing challenges facing people all over the world in the aftermath of the First World War, but the reader is short changed by the anodyne solutions put forward by the author that leave him hankering after answers that simply aren't forthcoming.

5

Setting Tales upon the Truth: *Three Go Back, The Lost Trumpet* and *Gay Hunter*

Instead of holding up a mirror to social reality and to the even more intimate reality of his own past experiences as he did in his first two novels, subsequently Mitchell turned to the more lightweight form of the imaginative romance. The metafictional rationale behind this new mode of approach slips in retrospectively to *Gay Hunter*, his final published romance, in which the shamanic Old Singer of the Folk who embodies and captures in words the idyllically simple lifestyle pursued by the primitive hunter-gatherers of the utopian world of the future defines the bardic function of the Singers: 'They set tales upon the truth, to make it more true' (*GH*78). 'Truth' isn't a relative term, and Mitchell fails to explain exactly what he means by it, but this is a workable enough conception of an inventive fable-style narrative with a universal moral set at its heart. In his own fantasies Mitchell creates more immediately pleasing lo-fi escapism subliminally fashioning optimistic themes about humankind's past and/or future and, more obliquely, about his present. The first two novels of this kind constitute hectoring libertarian parables that in the final analysis are little more than mechanistic vehicles for the promotion of Diffusionist dogma, but the final title, *Gay Hunter* itself, has a more urgent political message related to the louring European menace of fascism.

These novels, passed off by Mitchell himself as lighter pulp fiction, can be read nowadays as amusing speculative fantasies testifying to the enduring influence of Wells, and while in many respects they constituted comparatively easy ways of ticking boxes in contracts made with publishers for multiple titles, they are never devoid of purpose. Collectively, these three novels can be classified as proselytising fiction in offering pointed discourse addressing testing issues about human nature and forging direct links with contemporary society, but thematically over the piece the volumes progress away from gentle utopian idealism towards a more grounded concern with topical political developments. The two novels pursuing the popular fantasy trope of time travel, *Three Go Back* and *Gay Hunter*, are models of Christopher Booker's archetype of Voyage and Return, where the protagonists' unexpected transportation to an alien setting proves revelatory on their return to normality. The magical realism of *The Lost Trumpet*, meanwhile, is a classic example of Booker's definition of The Quest, where the heroes' mission leads through adversity to personal redemption and self-knowledge.[1] Mitchell's fantasy was lightweight but enlightening.

THREE GO BACK

The earliest imaginative romance *Three Go Back*, published in January 1932, is the most naked attempt by the author to fulfil his publisher's demand for sellable fiction capable of cashing in on the popular appetite for escapist distraction from the ills of the 1930s. The storyline is an amusing prehistoric fantasy revolving around a timeslip affecting the three protagonists chosen as representatives of modern times (a typically liberated Mitchell firebrand, a pacifist and an arms manufacturer), passengers on an airship catapulted back 25,000 years to an old Stone Age Atlantis appearing in the middle of the Atlantic. Mitchell indulges his powers of imaginative description to nurture the reader's suspension of disbelief, and he has great fun creating the unspoilt landscape of lost Atlantis and the spontaneous, subtly promiscuous lifestyle enjoyed by the pre-civilised inhabitants in an Eden tarnished only by the presence of savage Neanderthalers and the threat of the approaching Ice Age; in fact the plot proved raunchy enough to warrant censorship on republication in the United States a full decade later. Melodrama is introduced judiciously to spice up the storyline, in the night-time attack by lions, the mammoth hunt, threat of the Morlock-like Neanderthals, Clair and Sinclair separately becoming lost, the lurking wolf pack and the closing battle with the rabid Neanderthals.

Most productively, the imaginative projection of the contemporary protagonists into the prehistoric past allowed the author to dramatise one of the key tenets of Diffusionist theory, that primitive man was naturally a kindly and generous inhabitant of a pre-civilised Golden Age. Clair Stranley's ready immersion in the natural codes of behaviour of this undeveloped society reflects Mitchell's residual belief in the enlightened capacity of the female sensibility to oppose repressive norms.

In his opening address to RL Mégroz Mitchell dismisses his yarn as a playful 'holiday from more serious things', but the opening chapters especially forge a strong link with contemporary reality, making reference to the lingering death of Clair's lover in the trenches in France, charting the mounting tension around the rearmament of the major powers, particularly Germany, and doing just enough to keep the menace of the contemporary world in mind. The opening pages of the book have a shocking topicality conveyed through the idealised figure of Keith Sinclair, rumoured to have been deported from Germany following an anti-militarist intervention at a public meeting in Berlin. There he's said to have condemned the slaughter on the Western Front and denounced Sir John Mullaghan as well as 'Frau Krupp' – real-life industrialist Bertha Krupp, a key figure in the rearmament of a resurgent Germany in the run-up to the Second World War. Sinclair's anti-war invective articulates Mitchell's chief political fears at this early juncture of the 1930s, as Clair learns:

> [He] Says that another war's inevitable with the present drift of things and that it's up to the common people to organize and shoot down or assassinate their militarists and politicians at the first hint of it. (*TGB3*)

The pained reconstruction of atrocities recorded in humankind's past is one of the dominant memes of Mitchell's writing, and Keith Sinclair's tortured imaginings of the gross cruelties and perversions still to come in human history significantly features grim references to both the mass crucifixions of Spartacus's followers by the Romans and of Caesar's brutal reprisals against Vercingetorix's captive army (*TGB*116). Sinclair's distress patently is the author's own, and Mitchell's disturbing historical perspective is capped towards the end of the book by a more urgent condemnation of the 'lie about the everlastingness of rich and poor' and the less conspicuous afflictions of modern times, with the victims portrayed 'chained and gagged and brutalized, begging in streets, cheating in offices, doing dirty little cruelties in prison wards' (*TGB*194).

The rhetoric of Diffusionism laying the blame for these problems en bloc at civilisation's feet is fairly crudely trotted out through pacifist Keith Sinclair's developing historical awareness, set out to challenge the conventional evolutionist depiction of history as a smooth progression from primeval bestiality to civilised gentility. However, the most convincing element of Mitchell's challenge to historical orthodoxy revolves around his lyrical powers of description harnessed to celebration of the natural world and of the arcadian form of existence enjoyed by the ancient hunters; as Clair remarks: 'Those primitives of the Old Stone Age – they had some elemental contacts with beauty that we've lost for ever' (*TGB*61–2). Appositely, the novel is saturated in allusions to classic nature poetry, by Shelley, Tennyson, Morris and Rossetti, and Mitchell's original nature imagery is strikingly immediate, anticipating his representation of Chris Guthrie's nature-loving sensibility in *Sunset Song*. As lapsed socialite, Clair's ritualistic detoxification in the bucolic bastion of the past emulates Mitchell's own imaginative return to the rusticity of his upbringing, and the Scottish inflections creeping in to Clair's Stone Age idyll – to whin burning in summer, to swimming in the North Sea, to curlews calling – are harbingers of a new creative pathway that he was already edging towards.

THE LOST TRUMPET

Although it followed hard on the heels of *Three Go Back* in July 1932, *The Lost Trumpet* marked a noticeable advance in the author's technical skills and in the ambit of his ambition, especially in the fleeting experimentation with the modes of fable and allegory, which in the dynamic infusion of realism with fantasy broadly categorises the novel as what today is commonly termed magical realism. The novel's popular appeal is flagged up in its metafictional description as 'a boy's treasure-tale' (*LT*257), and the light-hearted murder-thriller-cum-fantasy-adventure-cum-travelogue set in contemporary Egypt proves highly readable in its deployment of the form of The Quest, here in pursuit of the talismanic Old Testament relic reputed to have brought about the collapse of the walls of Jericho.

Mitchell resurrects Anton Saloney from the *Polychromata* series for his curtain call as narrator, and the novel exploits the exotic fictional realm that he had created in his early stories. Aside from his irritating pidgin English, Saloney is a reassuringly urbane front man, and his affecting romance with the White Russian princess Pelagueya Bourrin also gives Mitchell the chance to add political heft to the novel when Saloney introduces her to the underbelly of backstreet Cairo, away from the tourist track. Early on in the book Saloney had established the ambivalence of the setting, vividly recalled by the author, as a semi-romantic meeting place of indigenous peoples and colonialists and tourists, but his insider's tour shocks his privileged guest out of her social complacency and into a desire to change things for the better, with the guide's sharply ambivalent portrayal of 'Cairo in horror and Cairo in loveliness' (*LT*121) opening out to embrace a vision of worldwide destitution and inequality:

> I thought of the starving miners in the English coalfields and the long queues of the unemployed there; the serfs on England's green and pleasant land. And were not the Gault monies invested in France? – France, with its rat-like peasant life, its bitter strugglings as of rats in a sewer. And no money in investments was static, these days of International Banks of Settlements. In German chemical works – who knew? – there were pallid young folk accruing dividends on that money of hers; on tramps at sea, with guano from the Peruvian islands; in Italy, with its comic State ferocities and its hunger-line industrial workers. (*LT*130–1)

This is certainly not fantasy by any conventional terms, and Pelagueya introduces a fresh dimension to the novel with references to Soviet authors such as Pushkin, Lermontov and Gorky being accompanied by more contemporary political allusions, expressly a sardonic portrayal of Stalin, already in power for a decade, cast as 'a Georgian peasant in the Kremlin, trampling underfoot everything clean and sweet' (*LT*133).

Mitchell expands the social mix of his central characterisation to a cross-section of six people representing 'humanity in little' (*LT*263). While this appears a bit formulaic, Marrot's Marxism adds some political nous to the proceedings and the nihilism of the artist Esdras Quaritch gives the theme a bracing modernist vigour – arguably too much so for the glib Diffusionist solution, concentrated into the mantra declared by Dr Adrian to *'be your essential self'* (*LT*139; italics in original text). However, realistically Adrian goes on two pages later to express the author's own reservations about the practical limitations of Diffusionism, describing the historical doctrine as a diagnostic tool allowing for the apprehension of the problems inhibiting human progress without presenting an actual cure. The snatch of the demonstration of the Cairene Labour Union towards the end of the book restores a welcome sense of political pragmatism, and the collective epiphanies of the individual protagonists at the end following the transformative sounding of the trumpet offers a fairly down-to-earth range of political or pseudo-political responses to modern problems, with Saloney and Pelagueya returning to Soviet Russia and the Communist Dream, Huebsch returning to the commune from his past in Jerusalem, Marrot going back to his crusade in America and Quaritch and Auslag staying on to work with the poor in the streets of Cairo. Despite the magic wake-up call, evidently the solutions to society's ills still lay in the people's hands.

GAY HUNTER

The two-year interval that elapsed before the publication of *Gay Hunter* is most evident in the novel's bluntly anti-fascist theme. Indeed, Mitchell's final romance skilfully blends the ravishing poetic evocation of natural harmony from *Three Go Back* with the contemporary political mettle of *The Lost Trumpet*. Published in May of 1934, chronologically *Gay Hunter* falls in between the two classics of British dystopian fiction, Aldous Huxley's *Brave New World* from 1932 and George Orwell's *Nineteen Eighty-Four* from 1949, and Mitchell's fable of 'ruined earth Britain' clearly has shed the earlier influence of Wells and bears favourable comparison with both Huxley and Orwell. Mitchell's arresting portrayal of a nightmare society of the future carrying the ills of the 1930s to an imaginative extreme that dramatises the systemic undermining of the freedom of the individual at the hands of mendacious global oligarchies marks this out as his outstanding fantasy.

The inscription to American author and journalist Christopher Morley claiming that 'this book has no serious intent whatever' but is 'written for the glory of sun and wind and rain, dreams by smoking camp-fires, and the glimpsed immortality of men' is again not strictly true. Mitchell's plan to waylay the unwary reader rested on a fantasy scenario that this time round is much more than *Three Go Back*'s light celebration of nature and natural man. Granted, Mitchell again employs a female protagonist predisposed, as her name indicates, to empathise with the simple, sensuous – and sensual – lifestyle of the hunters whose outlook sets up a familiar confrontation between their spontaneous humanity and the corruption of modern civilisation, damned in the very opening chapter as 'this for which men had sold their birthright' (*GH*5). However, this is quickly capped by the indictment of contemporary society trotted out in Gay's summation of bleak news stories from the press, with the climactic allusion to 'the beasts and savages of civilisation gathering under the swastika flag' (*GH*10) appearing especially menacing.

Mitchell propels Gay 20,000 years into the future by means of a rather corny plot device based on the pseudoscientific theory of 'serial time' propounded in 1927 by JW Dunne (of greater contemporary use to writers of science fiction than to scientists), but he's more successful in harnessing his intimate knowledge of his chosen setting of the Wiltshire Downs and the Chilterns all the way to 'the Shining Place' of London to anchor the action. Mitchell's last romance in fact skilfully fuses the two pre-eminent dystopian genres, of environmental disaster and political cataclysm: oligarchical tyranny has brought death and destruction to mankind, as a result plunging the world into a primordial reversion. Ever mindful of the social destitution prevailing in the metropolis that he had directly experienced in his earlier life, Mitchell takes personal delight in envisaging the ghostly Armageddon of London left following the apocalyptic clash between the Hierarchs who achieved autocratic rule in Orwellian War States and the enslaved Sub-Men whose revolt brought about the end of this totalitarian dystopia, with the stern reference to the destructive force of 'atomic bombs' proving forbiddingly prophetic (*GH*86). Mitchell again indulges his imagination in developing the fantasy of a regenerative England roamed by predators: condors, bears, jaguars, lions, giant sewer rats. Disappointingly, though, the central complication of the march of the Folk on London with its sophisticated weaponry manned by Gay's time-travelling companions, the fascist diehards Major Ledyard Houghton, formerly an officer in the Fascist Defence Corps, and Lady Jane Easterling, aristocratic patroness of the local fascist cell, is strangely wanting in tension. The twin deaths of the fascist leaders is sketched too lightly, due perhaps to the author's liberal proclivity for forgiveness, as Gay represents them as 'no more than victims of their one-time environment and education and social caste; and the aberrant culture that companioned that caste in the days of its economic straits' (*GH*161). In Mitchell's lifetime, however, fascist ideology had yet to attain its most repugnant manifestations.

As the protagonist, Gay begins as the archetypal 1930s siren in the mould of Mitchell's previous fiction heroines, combining elements of idealised sex goddess and feminist cipher, but she develops fascinating similarities with Chris Guthrie, from the very exposition capturing her in contemplation of the world below the Wiltshire Downs that cribs Chris's habitual retreat from the world in *Sunset Song*. By embracing the simplicity of her natural 'idyll', Gay makes a commitment to a life of elemental immediacy in which romance and physical love are prominent, set against the evanescent thinking of human history that had vexed Chris in *Cloud Howe*, as she apprehends 'all mystic philosophies and hopes as the play of diseased reflexes only' (*GH*55). Following humanity's degeneration, as related by the ancient recorded Voice, nature again proves restorative, and at the heart of the book Mitchell uses Rem as the shamanic Singer of the Folk to construct 'a triumphant paean', a lushly neo-pagan hymn commemorating the lasting restorative fertility of nature (*GH*99–100). The resemblance with *Sunset Song* is even more prominent in Book Two when Mitchell cites Heraclitus to help Gay to articulate her 'Philosophy of Change' in an extended disquisition revolving around the central thesis propounded by Chris Guthrie, that 'nothing endures'. Gay's self-analysis in fact describes Chris's evolution throughout the trilogy in terms that echo the Scots heroine's most intimate introspection:

> You grew from a child to a girl, to a woman, and in your growing you grew up within you this strange, delicate instrument of judging and assessing and creating – an instrument fine and keen and lovely ... . And presently it rusted and fell to fragments. (*GH*142–3)

Gay's reverie finally arrives at a sobering vision so typical of Mitchell, dominated by a metaphorically uncaring God:

> Nothing endured. The very planet that was man's – somewhere in the deeps of time death awaited it, death waited on all life that ever was, the flickering of a little flame in the dark wastes of space presently to be quenched by God as a hasting hand a taper. (*GH*143)

Following the destruction of London with its symbolically dissolute Tower of the Phallus in a rather conveniently conceived volcanic eruption, Gay even invokes the romance of 'life like a song' (*GH*178), attaining a state of grace in which she apprehends the organic symbiosis existing between the hunters and their environment. This climaxes in a stirring natural epiphany that she experiences that smoothly meshes with Rem's last visioning, as a pantheistic soothsayer, of 'the Paean of all life', in which Mitchell's tumbling natural imagery generates a sense of personal rhapsody (*GH*181).

Mitchell's fable has a pointed political dimension also, represented even more strongly through the sympathetic persona of his heroine. Where Houghton's clichéd right-wing principles are jingoistic and authoritarian, Gay's sympathies, like Chris's focalisations, are emotional and deeply felt, concentrated on 'all the poor folk labouring at filthy jobs under the gathering clouds of war and an undreamed tyranny', producing a nightmarish vision of the world imploding, ending as 'one great pounding machine, pounding the life out of humanity, making it an ant-like slave-crawl on an earth turned to a dung-hill of its own futilities' (*GH*15). Subsequently Mitchell's heroine condemns the scientific futurism of 'a machine-made world and machine-made humans' (GH31–2), accusingly attributed to 'the younger Huxley' himself, author of *Brave New World*, in which humankind is ruled by destructive technocracies ruled by 'insane creeds'; abruptly reverting to the contemporary world, the topical name-checking forging the reality of the present offers no reassurance whatsoever as Mitchell develops her speculation on the future fate of prominent contemporary figures in the public eye: Roosevelt, Hitler, Mussolini, Stalin, Chiang Kai-shek, Pavlov, Einstein (*GH*32).

Partly in keeping with his Diffusionist sympathies and partly conditioned by his steadily mounting radicalism, Mitchell's references to art and artists acquire an increasingly impatient air. As a romantic novelist caught up in a nature idyll, Gay thinks of herself as something of an anachronism in the grand scheme of things, and her self-reproach about her value in modern society expresses by extension her creator's growing conviction of the instrumental function of his own work, and of its necessary subordination to more pressing social and political priorities:

> Life an eternal picnic – it was the kind of thing that sick little imaginative novelists had dreamt of in the smoke and squalor and the unemployment queues of the fourth decade of the twentieth century. (*GH*59)

Mitchell undervalued *Gay Hunter* within his own corpus, perhaps mistaking the relative ease of its composition and its populist fiction genre as evidence of its lack of substance. As a political parable, though, his final English novel directly anticipates the celebrated visionary dystopian fiction fashioned by Orwell more than a decade later. The Old Singer's explanation of the Singers' bardic role in their simple society provides a perfect analogy for Mitchell's own achievement in this, his most sophisticated romance, and indeed in the genre as a whole: 'They set tales upon the truth, to make it more true' (*GH*78).

6

Haunted by Horrors: *Image and Superscription* and *Spartacus*

Mitchell provided a vital key to his whole creative aesthetic in the course of a letter written in 1933 at the height of his powers to his friend Helen Cruickshank, in which he confesses to being troubled by inner demons:

> It's going very well, in spite of the pathological horrors. Or probably because of them ... . Yes, horrors do haunt me. That's because I'm in love with humanity. Ancient Greece is never the Parthenon to me: it's a slave being tortured in a dungeon of the Athenian law-courts; Ancient Egypt is never the Pyramids: it's the blood and tears of Goshen; Ancient Scotland is never Mary Queen: it's those serfs they kept chained in the Fifeshire mines a hundred years ago. And so on. And so with the moderns: I am so horrified by all our dirty little cruelties and bestialities that I would feel the lowest type of skunk if I didn't shout the horror of them from the house-tops. Of course I shout too loudly. But the filthy conspiracy of silence there was in the past! – and is coming again in Scotland, in a new guise, called Renaissance, and Objectivity, and National Art and what not. Blithering about Henryson and the Makars (whoever these cretins were) and forgetting the Glasgow slums ... .[1]

When he observes 'of course I shout too loudly', Mitchell is presenting overstatement as a central feature of his writing, founded in the core belief that the artist has a moral obligation to confront the issue of human suffering as a matter of priority, and to place it at the very heart of his modus operandi. This grim purposefulness is fuelled by compassion for the downtrodden subaltern classes, the eternal victims of the 'horrors' plaguing human history; the almost neurotic concentration on human suffering came straight from Mitchell's heart, and writing about such unconscionable events provided a measure of catharsis for author and reader alike, as well of course as promoting a radical political response.

IMAGE AND SUPERSCRIPTION: A NOVEL

Both *The Thirteenth Disciple* and *Image and Superscription* follow the classic narrative archetype defined as one of the seven basic plots by Christopher Booker as Rebirth,[2] in which the force of good epitomised by the zealous hero triumphs over the threat posed by malevolent forces. In both of these early Mitchell novels, however, the redemption won at the climax is unconvincing. The author had plundered the original version of *Image and Superscription* for the Scottish elements of *The Thirteenth Disciple*, but the redacted typescript was now resurrected largely as a convenient stop-gap to fill a slot in his hectic publishing schedule contracting him to produce three conventional novels and three Scottish novels within the space of three years. Having stripped out the Scottish content, Mitchell hurriedly revamped *Image and Superscription* to fill out the original plan afresh, with the distinctly un-Scottish protagonist Gershom Jezreel being charted making a way through the hardships encountered in his childhood and early adulthood to find redemption finally in his romantic tryst with Ester Caldon, which signals renewal of their faith in humanity's ability to overcome life's misfortunes.

The author himself was unhappy with the book, but while it is undeniably very bitty (which is the root of its failure to earn re-publication), it has much to commend it. Once again Mitchell can be seen tinkering with narrative form, creating a distinctive first-person voice, ostensibly captured in a journal penned by his protagonist, with stilted phraseology loosened up syntactically by its inclusion in rambling compound sentences reminiscent of the innovatory Grassic Gibbon style unveiled the year before in *Sunset Song*. The narrative also has a vivid picaresque rush, jumping episodically from Chatham to Palenque, the Gulf of Mexico, Missouri and various European locations from Paris to Mitchell's home area of Welwyn, disclosing along the way scenes of the utmost cruelty from past and present.

Unfortunately, the vapid symbolism that brings *The Thirteenth Disciple* to a close is attenuated throughout *Image and Superscription*, pre-eminently in the Diffusionist-leaning anthropological theorising trotted out by George Shaw, Andrew Mellison and, later, by Gershom himself in their exotic travels in Yucatán. Locked in to his own study of the ancient Maya at this point, Mitchell makes over-generous use of his historical researches in his latest novel, which becomes a hollow medium for promoting Diffusionist polemic.

There are some intriguing parallels with Mitchell's best novels, in the characterisation of Gershom's tyrannical father who brutalises the warmly affectionate mother and in the protagonist's hard-won sympathy for a reviled figure of paternal authority who himself is subject to reappraisal as victim of a fanatical religious code and of the sheer grind of overwork; the strained relations dramatised within the Guthrie household at Blawearie hadn't receded far into the past. Furthermore, Gershom's partial recovery from the harrowing effects of the war at the Somme on his return to the farm he has inherited in Minneapolis echoes Chris Guthrie's retreat from war's personal ravages to the sanctuary of her 'fiere' of the Land. In addition, Gershom's philosophical understanding edges towards Chris Guthrie's vision of humankind's accommodation by the ever-changing universe all around us, as he ruminates:

> Life was no flower, it was mindless, the crawling of a mindless fecundity, changing and passing, changing and passing. Man was a beast who walked the earth, snarling his needs and lowing his fears, and with other beasts he would perish and pass, a ripple on the cosmic mind that itself was mindless ... . (IS193)

Gershom Jezreel is a familiar campaigning Mitchell hero committed to the quest for some means of helping humankind to climb from the moral morass that it's been mired in. His early sense of disillusion is typically deeply entrenched as he rejects his father's devoutness in his childhood and gravitates towards an atheist philosophy pitting Darwin's science against the unthinking creationism espoused by his father. His life experience repeatedly exposes him at first and second hand to some of the most eviscerating scenes imaginable, the most powerful of which recreate traumatic episodes from man's past and from the present day. Gershom's musings in the lost city of Palenque midway through the book, on time, on ancient history, on humanity's insignificance, throws up a pivotal passage in which the protagonist reflects with gruesome compulsion on Caesar's unemotional patrician record of the Roman conquest of Gaul and of the vile physical retribution inflicted on their captives. Gershom's transfixed abhorrence at the barbarity of the soldiers' systematic amputation of the Gauls' hands is very much a projection of the tortured imagination of the author of the forthcoming historical novel *Spartacus*, hypnotically drawn to the sufferings of the slaves at the Romans' vicious means of subjugation:

> It made you go white, you closed tight your eyes, but again you'd go back, read on, nobody had ever felt it as you, Caesar wrote of it cool and quiet, and his English editors penned calm notes, it was right, it was just, it was nothing. Nobody had ever seen it as you, the blood, how it spouted in a red-black stream, spouting from a dozen pipettes, from the axe-sliced arteries, as the hand of the Gaul fell limp from the block and the stump was thrust spouting in the bubbling pitch. Nobody but you had heard the gruntings of agony, the screams of the weak, or thought of the horror and fear on the faces of the men who waited by the block for their turn, and the cold, dense faces of the Romans themselves, the axes growing blunter and blunter at each stroke till at last they'd to hack and rehack ere a hand came off … . (IS119–20)

The account of Gershom's experience of the war on the Somme is recreated with comparable harshness, involving the desperate escape from the barbed wire in no man's land followed by brief rehabilitation back in Aberdeen, an episode that condemns the war by the more understated means of a gentle set-piece describing a casual meeting between Gershom and a young woman struggling to come to terms with the death of the kindly figure of her father at the beginning of the conflict. Mitchell's description of Gershom's return to the theatre of war with the French Foreign Legion fully captures the terrible beauty of modern industrialised warfare, and he skilfully coaxes pathos from the greater tragedy of the smaller scene as he focuses on the discovery by Gershom's patrol of the shocking evidence of a recent skirmish in which the peculiar positioning of the bodies of two Argyll and Sutherland soldiers indicates that one died vainly protecting his comrade. The domestic impact of this picture back home is delicately teased out as Gershom considers:

> Somewhere in Argyll or Glasgow there were still perhaps folk who believed that behind those notices of Missing these two lived unknown in some German prison, these two who had escaped even the prison of flesh. (IS213)

The single most shocking episode in the book, though, is taken from real life in contemporary America (as the author takes undue pains to state in a pointed footnote in the text) involving the description of a sadistic race killing carried out in Kentucky on a pregnant black woman – a quite sickening act that's all the more unnerving for its modern provenance.

Image and Superscription is even more arresting than its predecessors in its agonised delineation of historical and contemporary atrocities, and the shocking concentration on acts of barbarity and savagery that effectively wipes out the positive mood fabricated at the end may in fact be seen as an arresting staging post towards the more robust channelling of grisly images representing the historical excesses of ancient Rome in *Spartacus*, published just five months later.

SPARTACUS

The very act of choosing Spartacus as the eponymous hero of a novel was in itself a radical political statement. Marx, Lenin and Stalin had all seized on the commanding figure of the Thracian gladiator as the quintessential proletarian revolutionary, and Mitchell's imagination was completely won over by the historical tale of the most spectacular slave revolt ever staged when the initial prison break of seventy-four gladiators steadily attracted an army 60,000 strong that defeated the Romans in the field nine times and that within two years held the fate of Rome itself within its grasp.[3] Mitchell's research into the classical sources, of Plutarch, Appian and Sallust, was painstaking as ever, with his wife regularly helping him to sift through copious texts in translation at the British Museum. The extant historical material itself is patchy, but it offers the novelist scope to embellish it and to shape it to his own ends, affording Mitchell the ideal opportunity to work out his deep-seated vision of the traditional divisions afflicting human society that cause pain and torment for the ordinary people and to at least attempt to point towards political solutions for this persisting state of injustice. Specifically following the catastrophic left-wing failure of the General Strike that Mitchell had confronted head-on three months previously in *Cloud Howe*, his readership would have been desperate to latch on to any discernible ray of hope emerging from the historical novel.

In charting the legendary rebellion of Spartacus and his insurrection that brought the Roman Republic to the brink of defeat between 73 and 71 BCE Mitchell wasn't alone in modern times in tapping in to the political resonances of the whole episode; most famously, Karl Liebknecht and Rosa Luxemburg (regularly lionised in Mitchell's writing) had adopted the name Spartakusbund (Spartacus League) in Germany for their revolutionary cabal just after the First World War, and Stanley Kubrick's Hollywood epic from 1960, reproducing the radical political frisson of Howard Fast's 1951 novel, has done most to give the legend popular currency in modern times. Mitchell's portrait depicts the formation of a multi-ethnic force drawn from all nations led by a primitive dictatorship of the proletariat in a valiant and courageous freedom fight. His storyline has an irresistible drive as he traces the euphoria of the initial insurrection at Capua through the bloody campaigns in southern Italy to the final tragic defeat at Calabria, climaxing in the Romans' brutal reassertion of their authority in the mass crucifixions staged along the Appian Way. Spartacus himself is Mitchell's most memorable fictional character, an action hero straddling the thin line between man and myth and himself embodying the human qualities most cherished by the author – selflessness, empathy, courage, compassion. His metamorphosis is absolutely mesmerising as he morphs from simple military opportunist into a messianic freedom fighter who is both identifiably human and iconic, heralded as 'THE SLAVE himself' (S128) and 'the Voice of the voiceless' (S194). His own aggression latterly is tempered by a generous humanism embracing the mixed races among the slave army and even extending to include conquered foes. The author's cosmopolitan ideals thus are fully implicated in his historical scenario.

The classical legend of Spartacus provided Mitchell with the perfect radical narrative motif; the heady rebellion of the gladiators that came tantalisingly close to overthrowing the repressive Roman Republic seems custom made for him, with its concentration on the welfare of the underdog, on the condemnation of social and political oppression, on the heroic assertion of the human right to freedom and equality for all men. The epic sweep of the storyline calls Mitchell's imaginative powers fully into play, ranging vividly over the topography of the ancient Italian world, immersing the reader in rich period detail of the alien customs and culture of Rome, its multicultural society riven by endemic political corruption and dysfunctional principles of hierarchy and privilege. Moreover, Mitchell had learned from the intensive practice that he'd had by this time in writing narrative. The structure is functionally straightforward, divided into six equal sections, each of which is subdivided into modest subchapters in a compellingly linear storyline. And while the reader is bombarded with a quite bewildering wealth of detail, about people, places, events, races, customs, and beliefs, Mitchell deftly steers a way through the build-up of information with judicious foreshadowing, reinforcement and summarising of cardinal points. The prose style used throughout is formal to the point of archaism, the biblical simplicity of diction, imagery and syntax imbuing the narrative with a gravitas that at face value seems entirely appropriate to the classical subject matter. Mitchell reins in the narrative awkwardness contrived in the *Polychromata* stories, building specifically on the old-fashioned cadence of Neesan Nerses's chronicle, retaining the convoluted compound sentences simply connected with multiple 'ands' and converting modern vocabulary to more archaic locution.

Leslie Mitchell's boyhood passion for history encompassed pulp romances as well as more substantial works by notable writers of historical fiction like Sir Walter Scott. In adulthood he had a soft spot for Flaubert's *Salammbô* (1862), the historical novel set in Carthage during the third century BCE, which provided a model for his own visceral representation of the violent past. Contemporary inspiration came from Naomi Mitchison's achievements in the field of the historical novel, with Mitchell at various times singling out for special praise her novels *The Conquered* (1923) and *The Corn King and the Spring Queen* (1931) as well as the short story collections *Black Sparta* (1928) and *The Delicate Fire* (1933).

All the right ingredients were in place, then, and Mitchell's final reconstruction of life in the Roman Republic is thoroughly convincing – quite disturbingly so – although it involves a familiar binary simplification of the moral norms prevailing between the 'civilised' demagogues and the freedom-seeking oppressed. Mitchell doesn't shirk from depicting the full brutality of the age, which provides a platform for the dramatisation of the radical political force required to combat the established rule of oppression. As an impassioned advocate of moral principles rather than a student of Marxist philosophy, his novel may be interpreted as the imaginative promotion of bloody class warfare led by a Leninist figurehead in the universal search for the ideal of complete social freedom proffered by the millennium. The skills of the novelist put wind in the hair of the political vision, while the historical perspective allows for elliptical addressing of contemporary concerns. Realistically dramatising the friction simmering within the pluralist society of the slaves' camp and indeed the questionable ethics of certain of the slaves' most reprehensible actions, nevertheless Mitchell builds up the political credibility of this revolutionary movement. Beneath the petty squabbling there's a mutual recognition among the slaves of their common bond as a cognate class. Early on in the proceedings, in fact, this socio-political entente is seen to triumph over the fiercest religious differences, promoting a rapprochement between Gershom ben Sanballat and Kleon, Jew and Gentile respectively, and subsequent feuds are largely forgotten in the face of the one overriding purpose.

The author doesn't gloss over the harsh reality that bloody class warfare is a necessary preliminary to the achievement of the millennium; as Kleon cautions bluntly, 'we must destroy before we build' (S87). However, Mitchell makes it clear that Spartacus is no avenging angel and that the slaves aren't fighting for vengeance or for political supremacy but for their own freedom – and ultimately for a free world. The long-term objective of a classless society is recognised within both communist and anarchist theory, and Mitchell uses Spartacus himself to accentuate the greater humanity of their cause when he formulates the aim of a just society in which all class differences are abolished, declaring:

> I know nothing of the histories or plans of men, but there'll never be peace or the State unshaken, with women suckling their children at peace and men at work in the fields with quiet hearts, but that slave and master alike is unknown in the land. [...] If ever we build our slave state, there'll be no slaves in it at all. (S165)

While the noble ends that Mitchell promotes are most strictly anarchist, the unglamorous revolutionary means that he advocates in order to secure their fulfilment are conventionally Marxist; however, the historical distancing subtly makes the prospect of revolution appear more palatable, as well, paradoxically, as potentially more efficacious, even in the dark days of widespread hopelessness and despair in 1933.

The sensibility of Kleon, the eunuch whose physical emasculation has bequeathed a fierce intellectualism, memorably adds first-person intimacy to the narrative, and he is the cerebral vehicle representing the spiritual quest for meaning that accompanied the political upheaval between the world wars. Kleon's atheism prevails against the philosophy of Titul, a devout believer in the ancient god Kokolkh, and of Brennus, defined as the archetypal agnostic. Kleon sees the world as a scientific rationalist; he is the philosophical pragmatist who regards the universe as a physical phenomenon, with his brooding view of humankind proving extremely sobering:

> And it came on the eunuch, as so often, how strange it was that men should toil and moil on this little earth that knew them not – that knew only its winds and rains and the suns that ripened the crops, and the light and glow of the imaged sun, never the seedsmen or reapers. (S122)

As the classic Aristotelian deuteragonist, Kleon is second in importance only to Spartacus, and the author anchors the protagonist's radical political mission to Kleon's scepticism, anticipating similar philosophical collocations contrived a few years later by European left-wing philosophers such as Camus and Sartre and

Malraux. It's chiefly through Kleon's dying vision that Mitchell circumvents the negative impact of the slaves' defeat, crowning the dramatisation of the heroic potentialities of the ordinary people, called into play by acute social and political adversity, with a prophetic divination of the era of Christ's birth as a sign of the hope awaiting humankind. Ultimately, Mitchell's novel promotes with absolute conviction Kleon's abiding humanist ideal, of 'a dream of order on a planless earth, of endurance where all things meet and melt' (S80).

It's no surprise that *Spartacus* is Mitchell's most frequently translated book outside the trilogy, with Italian, Turkish and German editions appearing within the last ten years. In its sure-footed narrative approach and its ideological conviction Mitchell's best English novel has rightly acquired talismanic status as an emblem of the revolutionary movement in the twentieth century.

7

Distant Cousin Lewis Grassic Gibbon: *A Scots Quair* (*Sunset Song, Cloud Howe* and *Grey Granite*) and *Scottish Scene*

A SCOTS QUAIR: SUNSET SONG: A NOVEL

Mitchell's conventional English fiction is peppered with all sorts of fugitive Scottish elements, in characterisation, in setting, in language use, but having steadfastly carved out a niche for himself in the literary mainstream in London, the eager young author was reluctant to fly off at a tangent by producing a full-blown Scottish novel, particularly one intimately based on the remote rural world that he'd been brought up in far removed from the metropolis. In the Gibbon essay on 'The Land' from 1934 the author refers to 'my distant cousin, Mr Leslie Mitchell' (*Sm*83), which signalled his residual unease with juggling two public personas while recognising that the intellectual relationship remains secured by its fundamental bloodline. The invention of Lewis Grassic Gibbon, however, turned out to be absolutely inspired, matching the fecundity of Mitchell's creative ideas with an originality of expression that was both universally appealing and recognisably authentic.

The final stimulus for Mitchell to take the plunge came from a happy combination of factors, with closest to home his wife Ray and brother John both increasingly keen to see their own roots in a rapidly disappearing way of life memorialised. The publishing contract had actually been sealed more than a year before the book came out, when Mitchell signed a Memorandum of Agreement unusually tying him down to produce three novels (as opposed to the customary specification of a named book with two additional unnamed options) to be written by 'Lewis Gibbon', which confirms that the emergent trilogy was conceived as a single uniform entity.[1] The historic agreement, dated 23 June 1931, with the Grassic middle name added later by pen, secured the very modest advance of £25 (roughly half the contemporary average) – not a huge improvement on the niggardly £10 that he received for his first novel – reflecting the untested character of the new venture and the unknown identity of the new Scottish author. Mitchell's publisher at Jarrolds, Londoner Robert Hale, who stoutly championed Mitchell's cause with his superiors behind the scenes, provided the practical impetus for the Scottish trilogy: his awareness of the runaway success earned by AJ Cronin in May of 1931 with his first novel *Hatter's Castle* convinced him that Scottish fiction was a lucrative way for Jarrolds to go, while his intimate knowledge of, and belief in, Mitchell's abilities convinced him that he had the ideal credentials for the job. The use of the indefinite article in the trilogy's title may at first sight hint at a modest scale of authorial ambition, but the substantive old Scots word 'quair', meaning tome, historically endowed with regal gravitas by the seminal fifteenth-century Early Scots allegory *The Kingis Quair* of James I of Scotland, banishes any such notion. Gibbon's volume professes to be both grand and quintessentially Scottish, if not definitively so.

Having bought in completely to the London-centric prospect on British culture, Mitchell clung to a misplaced belief in the primacy of the literary mainstream. Nonplussed by the new direction that he was now following as a writer, consequently he was completely taken by surprise by the instant fame won by Grassic Gibbon. He happened to find himself perfectly in accord with the literary zeitgeist, following on from the resurgence in Irish writing witnessed at the beginning of the century and now linking in with the political devolution of interest away from London to the regions of Britain – including Scotland, where a thoroughgoing cultural renaissance was well under way. Mitchell, though, hadn't been especially interested in Scottish literature per se. Like most Scots, he had a working knowledge of Scottish history and of the poetry of Burns, and at school he declared a rather pretentious fondness for the novels of Sir Walter Scott. Beyond that, even his adult library boasted a modest Scottish shelf made up of titles mainly post-dating the advent of Lewis Grassic Gibbon and only rarely connected with what would be perceived as the Scottish literary tradition.[2]

Mitchell's service in the forces meant that he found himself lagging behind the times in terms of his general literary awareness, and he had been completely cut off from the bold new wave in Scottish writing. He would have been oblivious to the birth of 'Hugh M'Diarmid' in 1922 and to his later friend's initial exploits in laying down the fundamental principles of the new aesthetic in his polemical essays, in newly established periodicals providing a showcase for the kind of national initiative that he aspired towards and most memorably in producing in *Sangshaw, Penny Wheep* and *A Drunk Man Looks at the Thistle* in 1925 and 1926 the first ground-breaking exemplification of his creative aims.[3] Mitchell's own literary experimentation in the persona of Lewis Grassic Gibbon several years later appears to have been undertaken independently of these events. Always alive to fresh commercial possibilities, however, Mitchell proceeded to mine this rich new creative seam without ado, conscious of the opportunity that it offered for him not just to hedge his bets regarding the creative direction that he should follow but theoretically to double his output – and possibly also his earnings – without congesting the market.

While Mitchell was coming to the Scottish literary tradition as a virtual outsider, however, he would have become increasingly aware of the exciting stirrings being made in that direction following decades of couthy populism in the fields of poetry and fiction peddling parochial mawkishness and sentimentality as pumped out most commonly by the so-called 'kailyard' school of novelists. It was only in the early 1920s with Christopher Murray Grieve's appearance as the bold figurehead of a movement meriting capitalisation as the Modern Scottish Literary Renaissance, most adversarially under the pen name of Hugh MacDiarmid, that a more ambitious literary agenda emerged for Scottish writers, one that would renew the status of Scots language and literature by providing a robust forum for debate and innovation and that simultaneously would be alive to international influences while proving true to native Scots traditions – in practice a delicate balancing act for the writer to perform. As well as Grieve, there was a substantial diaspora of Scottish writers of varying degrees of public Scottishness plying their trade in and around London at the time, such as JM Bulloch, Compton Mackenzie, George Malcolm Thomson, Donald and Catherine Carswell, Naomi Mitchison and Edwin and Willa Muir; and in addition to maintaining regular contact with friends and family back in the Northeast, the Mitchells numbered several Scots among their closest friends in Welwyn Garden City and more broadly in the south, pre-eminently Harold and Jean Baxter (the latter of whom received the dedication of *Sunset Song*) at Wokingham.

While Mitchell himself owned to suffering severe bouts of the cultural cringe with regard to populist Scottish literature, he perpetually returned to Scottish subject matter and fiction modes throughout his writing career, from an early narrative experiment forging a hybrid of English and Scots that he trialled with the Grays to the introduction of Scottish characters to his stories and novels and of interludes set in various locations in Scotland – principally the Mearns. The abandoned typescript of *The Speak of the Mearns* – the most sustained precursor of *Sunset Song* – marks the most concerted attempt by Mitchell to compose fiction that was fully beholden to his Scottish heritage in style and substance, and Ray Mitchell of course was the staunchest advocate of this new turn in her husband's literary calling. She recalled how her husband required physically to distance himself from his Scottish background before he could achieve the desired artistic perspective from afar, both emotionally heightened and intellectually grounded by geographical detachment; but her intimate nightly review with the author of the almost hypergraphic progress of his typescript provided a vital validating link with the original source of his inspiration.

The 1930s was a uniquely rich period in the history of the Scottish novel, and *Sunset Song* was preceded by a number of highly promising volumes by Scottish writers initially signed up with London publishing houses – a trend that indicated a growing efflorescence in the genre. After the Scottish publishing boom following in the wake of the Scottish Enlightenment, from the middle of the nineteenth century the base of Scottish publishing had relocated from Edinburgh to London, with a resultant dilution and bastardisation of the Scottish element in terms of language and subject matter; for a decade the resurgence in Scottish writing revolving round the Scottish Renaissance of the 1930s gave rise in turn to a revival of a native publishing culture back in Scotland itself.[4] Most interesting potential novelistic influences on the birth of Lewis Grassic Gibbon were Nan Shepherd's *The Quarry Wood* from 1928, set in Mitchell's native Kincardineshire and now accepted as a classic novel of the Northeast, dealing with intimate life choices facing the female protagonist Martha Ironside that prefigure Chris Guthrie's growing pains. It's even more noteworthy that Mitchell knew of Ian Macpherson's *Shepherds' Calendar*, a rural novel published in 1931 set in the Glen of Drumtochty just a few miles due west of Arbuthnott in the remote uplands of the Mearns and chunked into sections named after the seasons, likewise featuring a protagonist torn between his farming background and his academic prospects.

Mitchell's highly resonant pen name digs back down into the family roots, with the author showing favour towards his mother in adapting his grandmother's name of Lilias Grassick Gibbon for most authentic effect. The adoption of a pseudonym had of course been an accepted strategy for authors to pursue for decades for a wealth of reasons, most notably as a political liberation for female writers, and in CM Grieve he had a ready model in his deployment of the pugnacious Scottish nom de guerre of Hugh MacDiarmid. Paradoxically, several critics were so taken in by the conspicuous realism of the representation of Chris Guthrie in the first Gibbon novel that they were convinced that the male pen name was a cover for a female author.

Within Mitchell's eclectic reading several key non-Scottish influences can be detected in the conception and execution of the Grassic Gibbon fiction also. Mitchell had access at his local libraries in both Glasgow and Hammersmith to FS Delmer's English translation from 1905 of *Jörn Uhl*, the most successful rural novel and the foremost model of *Heimatkunst* (regionalism) by the German pastor Gustav Frenssen from 1901. Similarities in social setting, characterisation and plot aren't compelling, though, and Frenssen's saga of peasant life in the Duchy of Holstein lacks the richness and depth of *Sunset Song* – but the novel conceivably gave Mitchell a gentle nudge in the right direction.[5] In addition, Erich Maria Remarque's anti-war novel

All Quiet on the Western Front (1929) helped Mitchell to formulate his own approach to the subject in the final chapter of *Sunset Song* and particularly to shape the individual responses of Long Rob of the Mill and Ewan Tavendale. The ambit of his literary aspirations that he constructed to frame his lasting plans for his trilogy in the essay 'Literary Lights' in fact travels well beyond Scotland in invoking his dream to disclose 'a new Melville, a new Typee, a Scots Joyce, a Scots Proust' (*Sm*124) and to bring the long-term aim to fruition to see the galvanising effect when 'a Scots Virginia Woolf will astound the Scottish scene, a Scots James Joyce electrify it' (*Sm*127).

Lewis Grassic Gibbon actually rests uneasily with the Scottish Literary Renaissance, whose major protagonists frequently, not unnaturally, pursued a nationalist political agenda in tandem with their cultural objectives. The author of *A Scots Quair*, *Niger* and co-author of *Scottish Scene* fits much more comfortably into the tradition of subaltern writers stretching back to Burns, Hogg and Galt whose voices had a radical political edge directly opposed to the privileged elite of Scottish society – and indeed committed to the active affirmation of basic humanitarian sympathies. Moreover, while the first Gibbon novel remains a landmark in Scottish literature, the author himself sets down a clear marker in the prefatory Note whereby he draws a parallel with a similar situation hypothetically facing a Dutch author regarding language use; the frame of reference is pan-European, cosmopolitan, universal.

Several of the ingredients of the novel itself had already been rolled out in Mitchell's published works: the heavily verbalised first-person focalisation, the strong female protagonist, the romantic storyline, the First World War setting, the highly moral charge, the radical political orientation of the theme. *Sunset Song*, though, is a fully extended act of remembrance and belonging on Leslie Mitchell's part, identifiably the book of a lifetime in which he plunges most deeply into his creative wellspring. It's also a statement of faith in human nature, in the importance of humankind securing a healthy relationship with the natural environment, and indeed less obviously a highly political tract by an unreconstructed revolutionary.

The passage of time has brought out the genius in Mitchell's aesthetic as a Scottish writer. His approach to language is unerringly sure-footed as the measured Grassic Gibbon lexicon reconciles universal intelligibility with pungent Scots cadence and diction. Scottish vernacular literature had become widely available in Victorian newspapers, culminating in classic novels of the Northeast, principally those by William Alexander, such as *The Authentic History of Peter Grundie* (1855), *The Laird of Drammochdyle* (1865) and *Johnny Gibb of Gushetneuk* (1869).[6] However, where these works confine the readers to a Doric strait-jacket constructed from the authors' minutely recreated phonetic transcription of real Buchan speech, the Gibbon style is a much more flexible instrument. Mitchell's Glossary for the American edition of the novel published in 1933 by the Century Company of New York was compiled with reluctance, as a fairly redundant support mechanism for a finely tuned narrative in which the context, in keeping with the author's published aims, suggests the meaning of unfamiliar words and idioms; the brevity of the list itself flags up just how little he actually uses in the book by way of traditional Scots vocabulary – amounting to just over a hundred words. The function of the Scots words, the author explains, is simply to sharpen expression by offering shades of meaning not available in formal English. His linguistic theory set out most clearly in the essay on 'Literary Lights' in *Scottish Scene* articulates his aim to strike a happy medium in his fiction style:

> The technique of Lewis Grassic Gibbon in his trilogy *A Scots Quair* [...] is to mould the English language into the rhythms and cadences of Scots spoken speech, and to inject into the English vocabulary such minimum number of words from Braid Scots as that remodelling requires. (*Sm*135)

Mitchell's ingenious resolution of the linguistic quandary inherited by the Scottish fiction writer facing the traditional fault line setting narrative and dialogue apart has reasonably been said to have paved the way for the demotic achievements of modern Scottish writers such as James Kelman and Irvine Welsh. Dialogue has been liberated by the abolition of quotation marks, a simple mechanism affording the speaker's discourse semantic and political parity with the contribution of the narrator – customarily the voice of authority. (Classics such as *Robinson Crusoe*, *Moll Flanders* and *Great Expectations* avoided this narrative schizophrenia through the authors' simple recourse to first-person narrative.) Formerly relegated to direct speech, the vernacular voice is now emancipated and grammatically and socially shares ownership of the narrative on an equal footing with the actual storyteller, whose power is already weakened by being distributed among a chorus of diverse personas. Furthermore, the representation of direct speech in italics as opposed to speech marks, the dispensation with the convention to accord new speakers a fresh paragraph and the dropping of intrusive apostrophes for Scots abbreviations all add to the sense of unity and coherence. Much of the appeal of the protean Grassic Gibbon style, bouncing from character to character in abrupt jump-cuts, is addressed to the eye rather than the ear: his adaptation of dialect words such as 'chiel' and 'quine' and 'braw', given his own stamp in their transformation into more universally recognisable 'childe' and 'quean' and 'brave', become normalised as anchors in the tumbling narrative. Within this lexicon Gibbon makes extensive use of simple conversational features incorporating introductory epithets ('Well', 'Now', 'So', 'And') and interjections ('faith!', 'feint the meikle') that bind the narrative together and simple repetition of phrases that serve especially to heighten the emotive impact at times of particular drama, particularly in Chris's life.

The effectiveness of Gibbon's flexible narrative mode belies its sophistication, in that it challenges the reader to keep pace with the rampant switches of persona that occur largely without warning, employing the generic 'you' pronoun (that subtly draws the reader in to a warm sense of inclusivity), sometimes delivering Chris's own stream of consciousness but often flitting from one narrator to another, often boasting distinctive features – young/old/male/female – and frequently unreliable in character, putting pressure on the reader to winnow the truth from an ironic accretion of gossip, half-truths, exaggerations and plain lies.[7] With its intimate tone, the fragmentary folk voice clearly comes from an insider who belongs to the Kinraddie community. As such, the narrator is both sardonic commentator and object of ridicule – in turns prudish, salacious, mischievous and irresponsible, and never anything less than engrossing. Gibbon takes liberties with punctuation, making a virtue of the comma splice to create extended heavily vocalised compound sentences that ramble and meander seemingly interminably. This also helps the narrative to maintain a brisk tempo, with sprawling ungrammatical sentences being connected in a seemingly haphazard fashion that lends an impressionistic, anecdotal spontaneity to the proceedings and builds up momentum in the narrative, descriptive and reflective passages.

Interwoven with this seemingly down to earth, thoroughly immersive verbal torrent is a rich vein of imaginative imagery that provides forensically sharp descriptions of people, places, actions, of sights, sounds and smells. The writer was clearly in his most creative mode, in his ultimate comfort zone. The potency of the imagery can be felt from paragraph to paragraph; it's especially well exemplified in the treatment of Chris's heightened awareness induced by the oxytocin rush immediately following the birth of young Ewan in 'Seed-Time', in which the tenderness of new motherhood is captured in her euphorically detailed description of her baby, with 'a face as small as though carved from an apple', 'a body as small and warm as a cat's' and 'a tongue like a little red fish in the little red mouth' (SS195). The perfectly apposite analogies bathe the whole scene with a beatifically pellucid glow. Absence sharpened Mitchell's powers of recall, and his reliving of the myriad effects of the seasons, of weather systems, of light and mirk and dark, of bird and animal life, of the ever-changing Mearns vista of fields and hills and woods and clouds comes flooding out with graphic precision as the author marshals his descriptive powers to the full to keep up with the flood of memories, lithely reflecting the tone and mood of the narrative. Similarly, his portrayal of the work of the farm prior to mechanisation afforded by the restriction of the novel's time setting to the period round about the First World War endows the story with a grounded simplicity. Descriptions of farming jobs throughout the agricultural calendar are exhaustive, although the metaphorical strictures of the chapter headings of The Song are often broken in order to fulfil the literal requirements of his narrative: for example, the fullest account of sowing actually appears in the section Ploughing (SS57) and Ewan's spring ploughing is most poetically realised in Seed-Time (SS175).

While Mitchell was building on earlier experimental approaches to narrative by modernists such as Joyce and Woolf and Faulkner, particularly in the development of stream of consciousness techniques, there's an effortlessness about his style that came from the easy flow maintained in the actual composition and that develops a rhythmic compulsion in the reading experience. The cleanness of the eighty-page fragment of the original folio typescript for *Sunset Song* preserved among Mitchell's papers, which is virtually identical to the published text, is indicative not just of the author's typically exacting working practice but of the fluency of composition. As he explained at the time, he set a daily target of eight pages, written in a rhythmic form of prose roughly similar to blank verse, which helped to keep the ideas on the move.[8]

The rhythm of the narrative isn't just embedded in the poetic patterning of the diction, though: it's also relentlessly anecdotal in its drive, replicating the to-and-fro of light conversational bickering producing waves of repartee repeatedly racked up to a climactic, frequently bombastic, wisecrack trumping all previous quips, as the folk voice riffs sardonically on anything seen, heard or, most likely, imagined. The default narrative style predicated on interactive local banter thus forms a chorus representing the generic mindset of the people, as well as simply charting the actions and events in the life of the community. In spite of the authorial shape-shifting, the tropes and themes at the heart of the Gibbon writings remain identical with those to be found in the Mitchell publications, but the literary vehicle is palpably different and much more convincingly 'real' – and certainly no less compelling, even, crucially, for readers from outwith Scotland. And of course it's important to appreciate the commercial benefits held out for an established author of adopting a new pen name and establishing a fresh new audience right throughout the English-speaking world when substantial hikes in bulk sales were required to earn the contracted incremental increases in royalties.

As has already been suggested, the Grassic Gibbon narrative style has momentous political implications also, as his liberation of the disembodied folk voice from the traditional constriction within speech marks is a cultural and political instrument for what is essentially a democratising initiative. The kaleidoscopic narrative, veering from persona to persona, specified and unspecified, invites the reader into the heart and mind of the community, affording access to the broad sweep of opinion rippling through it and reflecting the black and the white in the people's character as well as many of the shades of grey in between. Individually and collectively, the characterisation, as Chris metafictionally explains, is gloriously and authentically 'up-jumbled' (SS144). As Robert Colquohon declares in the sermon at the book's climax, the ordinary people as a whole traditionally had been deprived of the power to describe their shared experiences, to articulate the core values and principles that they held most dear and to represent their own cause. In the person of Grassic Gibbon, Mitchell does just this for his incorrigible protagonists, the subaltern class of Kinraddie.

Sunset Song is an intimate celebration of the bittersweet drollery of everyday life just as Mitchell had come to know it in his childhood at Auchterless and more fully in his adolescence in the Mearns. Keenly receptive to new ideas, his unique multifaceted narrative carries Faulkner's more disciplined polyphonic approach from *As I Lay Dying* to a more mottled, seemingly spontaneous, extreme, submerging the reader in an unrelenting maelstrom of community hearsay involving gossip, misunderstanding, distortion and invective shrouding the actual events that take place.

Mitchell pledged his mature art to the pursuit of radical political ends serving pressing social causes, and while *Sunset Song* is too often treated as a standalone book, the trilogy is holistically integrated to create a moral mandate of latent political intent in the first volume that becomes more overtly political in the tragic failure of the events surrounding the General Strike dramatised in *Cloud Howe*, finally culminating in the revolutionary urgency elicited by the desperate contemporary conditions represented in *Grey Granite*. It's important to emphasise *Sunset Song*'s status as a transportive historical novel within this schema. On publication the book was widely hailed as a narrative promoting a neo-pastoral alternative to an increasingly urbanised Scotland. Granted, the historical scene was only a decade and a half in the past, and yet experientially it was a world away, with the First World War providing an insurmountable interface with what had gone before. From publication the novel has gathered the allure of a quaint period piece, a nostalgic evocation of a golden past. However, within the author's grand design the rural world portrayed in *Sunset Song* is already obsolete and its distinctive culture and ethos have virtually disappeared. We can look backwards for guidance, but the concerns now lie with an entirely different kind of social order – first the industrial town, and second the modern reality of the city.

The setting of *Sunset Song* arguably has the strongest kinship with real life. Kinraddie is part of a matrix of place names encompassing a familiar cordon of real villages in the Mearns (Stonehaven, Kinneff, Auchenblae, Drumlithie and Bervie), adaptations of real farms (Netherhill and Upperhill for Nether Craighill and Upper Craighill, Peesie's Knapp for Birdyknap), and fabrications: Kinraddie itself seems a play on the county title of Kincardine while Blawearie appears a minor rearrangement of Balwearie, an area of Kirkcaldy situated to the south of the Mearns in Fife. Ray Mitchell's labelling of her husband's book as 'his story of the Reisk' was quite specific,[9] and the upland setting of Blawearie is plainly identifiable with that of his old family farm of Bloomfield. The description of Kinraddie Kirk (and the adjacent manse) is also based directly on the Church of St Ternan back at Arbuthnott, the trig thirteenth-century parish kirk perched on a promontory above the Bervie Water that Mitchell attended with his family from boyhood; the distinctive landmark was begging for incorporation within the novel (particularly the interior with its striking stained-glass windows and its strictly hierarchical layout), serving as an invaluable focus for the community, presented at Sunday worship in all its chequered humanity before the keen-eyed young observer in their midst.

Characterisation and plot are both greatly indebted to the local Mearns lore stored up by Mitchell from his Arbuthnott years and augmented from regular contact with family and friends thereafter. Many of the cameos were drawn from real life. As the quintessential crofter, John Guthrie shared the chief physical and temperamental attributes of James Mitchell (although they're carried to an extreme in the fiction, particularly in his Calvinist fundamentalism), while Lily Mitchell also reputedly had a subtle influence on the portraiture of Jean Guthrie. Most illustriously, the anarchic freethinker Long Rob Duncan was directly based on Ray's father Robert Middleton in more than their shared Christian name, while Chae Strachan resembled local roadman Charlie Smith in his highly vocal dedication to socialist politics – a disposition that was just as outlandish in Arbuthnott as it appears in Kinraddie. Some of the more farcical character traits also were traceable to the author's home area: Ellison, incoming Englishman on the make, was well known, as was Dallas with his physical quirk of his protruding 'lugs'; the anecdote about the 'daftie' whose shorthand note betrayed his inner resentment at his mistreatment by the wife at the farm where he was billeted was true; and the Dickensian caricature of the Reverend Stuart Gibbon, the minister who gives in to the temptations of drink and the sins of the flesh and who indulges in a bacchanalian jaunt to Aberdeen, was said to bear some relation to the minister who received his calling to Arbuthnott in 1921 – especially in the merry-making rail trip to the city.

The community of Kinraddie boasts all the protean potentialities of the most substantial family saga or serial, or most strikingly of a modern-day soap opera, offering up boundless possibilities for character development and interaction and for storylines evoking the whole gamut of dramatic moods from the comic to the tragic. The elucidation of the community dynamic operating in a typical country parish round about the First World War presents an engagingly familiar mix of people and a realistic array of character types involved in everyday activities punctuated occasionally by the extraordinary – principally linked with the war. The authenticity of this social milieu is further enhanced by the narrative's immersion in the cultural traditions, largely interwoven with local agricultural customs and practices, that Mitchell experienced himself at Arbuthnott and the surrounding area, from the rituals that had evolved in the conduct of Northeast funerals and weddings to the boisterous indulgence of the Harvest Home and low-key celebration of the New Year. Music, song and dance skip lightly throughout the local festivities represented in the novel, from the impromptu ceilidh instrumentation of Chae and Long Rob to the country dances such as the Schottische, Eightsome Reel and Petronella and the heavily Burns-based repertoire of songs and ballads rendered at Chris's wedding. Most memorably, the bagpipe dirge of 'The Flowers of the Forest', a seventeenth-century tune with modern lyrics by Jean Elliot commemorating the Scottish losses at the Battle of Flodden in 1513, the actual sunset song played by McIvor at the novel's finale at the Blawearie standing stones that metaphorically acts as a refrain throughout the novel and provides a musical motif for the tragedy mourned at the close, is on record as the lament played at the inaugural Armistice Day service held at Arbuthnott on 29 June 1919, the precise time when Mitchell had just returned home from his sacking in Glasgow. Leslie Mitchell would have felt the impact of the conflict creeping over life at home and then in Aberdeen just as he traced its sinister progress throughout Harvest, the final chapter in *Sunset Song*, and in the Epilude. The roll call of Arbuthnott's fourteen war dead whose names are engraved on the modest war memorial built in to the wall fronting the local village hall is no less moving for being concentrated into 'those four' lost in the Gibbon novel – Charles Strachan (Chae), James Leslie (anointed with Mitchell's own Christian names), Robert Duncan (Long Rob) and Ewan Tavendale.

Chris Guthrie is at the very heart of the novel, and while several of Mitchell's female acquaintances claimed that they saw themselves in her characterisation, she is a splendid bespoke creation moulded from the author's deepest creative desires and fictive requirements for his protagonist. Inevitably, several of his own experiences and his most pronounced characteristics coalesce in her portrait: the inner tension felt between her 'Scots' and 'English' personas, the profound affinity with the natural world, the guarded respect for formal education, the ambivalent relationship with the family patriarch, the seething humanitarianism and, most singularly, the defiant assertion of personal independence. It's largely through the novel's vibrancy as a bildungsroman, though, that it engages so profoundly with readers in their own journey through life, providing a universally identifiable index to the pleasures and pains of the human story, of growing up, of exploring the immediate environment, of integrating with family and community, of learning about the world, of falling in love and having children, of facing up to the utmost challenges posed by the deaths of loved ones.

Sunset Song has found an especially appreciative audience across the world in farming folk who could recognise the veracity of the author's portrait of the old farming ways;

however, it also appeals to readers hankering after imaginative refuge from the anxieties and complexities of modern life. To this extent, the novel is peddling nostalgia and its pull is a sentimental one; indeed the emotional impact of the book is irresistible – in tracing the romances between Will and Molly and Chris and Ewan, in the comedy, in the pathos, and in the heady bittersweet mixture of the two. Overall, Mitchell's restricted canvas lures the readers in and invites the willing suspension of their disbelief, particular geared towards coaxing wholehearted identification in the novel's default narrative with Chris Guthrie, in her turbulent development from adolescence to maturity, in her struggle to resolve her key life choices, in her tangled relations with her family and the community embracing them, in her romantic development and in her submission to the final collective capitulation to the implacable advance of all-conquering global forces – principally those of war and capitalist economics. The highly emotive nostalgia that the novel seems to offer is neither passive nor backwards looking, though, and in the haunting closing scene at the standing stones in the Epilude Mitchell pulls out all the stops to maximise its immediacy through its cinematic conception – in the lyrically familiar place setting, in the diminishing lighting effects created by the onset of the gloaming and in the musical soundtrack of the traditional bagpipe lament reinforcing the pathos of the tragedy being commemorated. The emotionality of these combined features brings the action to a crescendo, focusing in on the elegy delivered by Robert Colquohoun that crowns the narrative. Ultimately his sermon, rightly labelled 'just sheer politics' by the ingenuous narrator (SS261), firmly establishes the moral imperative to seek a robust political response to the tragedy that has unfolded, sustaining a powerful call to work for 'a new spirit' that will vouchsafe the homespun values that the dead victims personified: 'the kindness of friends and the warmth of toil and the peace of rest'.[10] The resolution of the first novel of the trilogy is in actual fact the ultimate cliff-hanger, pointing forward expectantly to the much more hard-edged political polemic of the subsequent volumes.

Despite the coruscating plot, the structure of the novel has of course built up to the climax, channelling the narrative expertly for the author's thematic ends. The Unfurrowed Field elucidates the moral and political theme to be drawn from the social realism of the intervening Song that, divided into increments denoting the key seasons in the agricultural calendar, of Ploughing, Drilling, Seed-Time and Harvest, reflects the rustic setting that the novel is submerged in, as well as metaphorically charting Chris Guthrie's physical, emotional, sexual and intellectual development. The Harvest chapter title acquires peculiarly negative connotations in light of the wholesale slaughter of the war traced in the final stages of the book that also takes the life of Chris's husband.

As he acknowledged in the prefatory note to the American edition of the novel, the author's structural approach makes extreme demands of his reader in plunging into what essentially constitutes a false start in the Prelude, which offers a pastiche of traditional overblown annals-style history. The early legend of Cospatric and the following aristocratic dynasties of Kinraddie reorientates the traditional social and historical perspective that panders to those in authority, presenting a breathless warts-and-all tour of the local seat of power down through the ages. In its sheer sketchiness Mitchell satirises the selectivity of such bloated narratives, although in his parody the protagonists themselves are represented as fallible to the point of ridiculous grotesquerie. The initial assumption of the Kinraddie lands by Cospatric de Gondeshil, a venal Don Quixote, is exposed as a cheap con-trick as he gains rich reward for sallying forth and killing a gryphon, a mythical creature that never had a physical reality and, just for good measure, he sets his heroic dissemblance in the night-time, putatively under cover of darkness. The high farce is archly maintained by Mitchell throughout the following mock-heroic saga of the Kinraddies' skulduggery and fraudulence, breezing throughout the Scottish wars of independence (pitched of course against the Scottish patriot Sir William Wallace), the Covenanting period, the French Revolution and the infamous land clearances. The madness of the final Cospatric scion brings the whole lineage to a suitably lamentable conclusion as the Meikle House falls into physical disrepair, the narrator relishing its final ruination in his graphic rustic simile, describing how it 'crumbled to bits like a cheese' (SS13).

Following the candid humanising of the upper echelons of Kinraddie society in the opening section of the Prelude, the prevailing voice that bosses the remainder of the narrative slams in, resolutely and defiantly subaltern in nature, declaring to all and sundry, 'but you were as good as they were' (SS12); the adversarial theme is flagged up from the very outset – and indeed the inclusional effect of the generic you broadens out this casual remark into a defining statement of intent, a revolutionary mantra for a whole social echelon. In the following narrative Mitchell dramatises and promotes the values inherent to the 'common', the ordinary people of the community, but it's not an idle exercise in passive nostalgia – as the Epilude makes abundantly clear in tracking the dreadful ravages of the war on the community of Kinraddie, capped by Robert's closing sermon, in which the author pulls out all the rhetorical stops to spell out with explicit directness the lesson to be learned from what has gone before.

One of the most telling reasons behind the extraordinary popularity of *Sunset Song* rests with the author's sensitive treatment of the romance between Chris and Ewan. Following the serial traumas of her upbringing and adolescence, with her mother's suicide and the poisoning of the twins, her brother's emigration and her father's lingering demise, the happiness that she's due is developed with captivating tenderness in Seed-Time. After their first jaunt to Dunnottar Castle their relationship is shown to be conducted eminently realistically, with avowed common sense alternately tempered with and assailed by youthful passion. Their mutual attraction is duly extended by their bonding in the daring sortie to rescue the horses from the electrical storm, which convinces Chris that they've reached a defining moment in their relationship. Mitchell thereafter underlines the decisiveness that distinguishes their brief courtship (as ever, a source of choice scandal locally), which smoothly leads on to the wedding on New Year's Eve, presented with consummate skill spotlighting the formal ceremony and its celebration to show the close-knit community of Kinraddie at its caring, sharing best. Approached tenderly again from Chris's interiorisation, there's tremendous psychological poignancy in Chris's fleeting hankering after her dead mother (SS155) and her longing for her absent brother Will (SS171), while the merriment submerges the reader in the author's exuberant recreation of Northeast tradition at its liveliest, laced with appreciable sentimentality, from the arrival of the guests generously armed with thoughtful wedding gifts through the touchingly simple ceremony. The meal merges into the speeches, and finally the reader is swept up into the gusto of the dance, affording a window into the traditional structure of such festivities. The singing that offers a temporary reprieve from the energetic reels and strathspeys subsequently offers further insight to the personality of the individual singers (SS168–70); Chris's turn is of course the most revealing, her choice of the lament of 'The Flowers of the Forest' acting as a personal anthem that has provided an outlet from her childhood for her social sympathies, firmly placed with historical victims. Finally, the physical consummation of their marriage is treated with a gentle simplicity; and Chris's pregnancy brings Seed-Time to an aptly sanguine close, with the latest stage in her archetypal journey as Everywoman being realised again in substantial terms reflecting the shedding of a persona and the welcoming of a new metamorphosis.

Sunset Song is one of the most eloquent fictional responses to the cataclysm of the First World War, although the war only appears in Harvest, the final chapter of the novel, and its impact is almost completely confined to the home front. The insular contentment of the newly-weds, with Chris now expecting their first child, is interrupted briefly by Chae's excitement at the declaration of war (SS191), and following the startlingly visceral account of Chris's experience of childbirth, Chris and Ewan are both protected from the news of the encroaching threat of the conflict abroad, which early on takes the life of the Upperhill foreman James Leslie, metafictionally endowed with the author's real Christian names in a striking act of literary self-immolation. The war becomes even more menacing with Chae's fiery decision to enlist and Rob's defiance of the local jingoists, including the minister, whipped into a patriotic frenzy by political propaganda. Rob's stance stands out for its incisive common-sense, his objections emulating Erich Maria Remarque's most swingeing anti-war criticism in *All Quiet on the Western Front*, published in English only three years previously. Admirably, Chris and Ewan are seen to remain aloof, 'douce and safe and blithe in Blawearie', prompting Chris to muse, 'content, content, what more could she have or want than the two of them, body and blood and breath?' (SS198, 204). Steadily, though, Mitchell tracks the increasingly invasive threat posed by the outside world, with Chae's first-hand account of the conflict reflecting his informed disillusionment with the war's objectives. The human cost in Kinraddie is now plain to Chae, but Ewan's skulking disappearance from Blawearie to join up in Aberdeen is hardly unexpected – although the wisdom of his decision is highly questionable within the ethical context that Mitchell has created, as Chris turns to young Ewan and to the land for emotional and spiritual relief.

Ewan's tragedy follows a classical Aristotelian pattern. His brutalisation, made manifest on his army leave where Chris is forced to hold him at bay with a knife, underlines the gravity of his *hamartia*, throwing his lot in with an alien cause that goes against everything that he believes in. By the time he has realised the error of his ways of course it's too late, and his fate is sealed following the vainglorious effort to return home to Chris at Blawearie. Chris's retreat to the succour of nature after her final set-to with Ewan, following on from Rob's shameful torturing as a conscientious objector at the hands of the vengeful authorities, reinforces his folly in rejecting her. Mitchell's sequencing of the closing events of the chapter is captivating, emotionally buttressing the pacifist message. Chris's farewell tryst with Rob – morally a hugely contentious act on the part of Mitchell's heroine – is an act endowed with symbolic status in heralding the passing of an era, and the author's handling of Chris's subsequent widowhood is absolutely crushing. The official telegram delivered the next day bluntly informing her of Ewan's death unleashes a torrent of emotions running the full scale of personal grieving from shock to anger and finally ending in denial. Chris's emotive understanding of the uselessness of Ewan's death rings resoundingly true within the novel's moral compass, however, offering a powerful indictment of the whole war effort sharply confronting her own benign rural world of Kinraddie with the orchestrated madness of the hostilities and with the mendacious political establishment that is responsible for it all (SS238).

Even before Chris learns from Chae of the real manner of Ewan's death, shot at dawn as a deserter, the reader is fully disposed to side with her searing denunciation of 'the world that had murdered her man for nothing, for a madman's gibberish heard in the night behind the hills' (SS239). Mitchell is reputed to have known of one specific instance of the implementation of the infamous British Army Act in Arbuthnott, where an unnamed recruit fell victim to the heinous policy of executing soldiers classed as deserters, principally as a deterrent, one of the most egregious wrongs of British military history, accounting for 312 named victims eventually granted retrospective pardon in Parliament in 2006;[11] the author's wrath can be fully gauged in his harrowing depiction of Ewan's fate. Ewan's final expression of regret, reported by Chae, confirms his returning sanity in a classic *anagnorisis* (SS242-3); Chris's subsequent fondling of Ewan's clothes, 'those clothes that had once been his, near as ever he'd come to her now' (SS243), points up the shocking finality of her personal loss. However, the closing scene of the chapter, and of The Song, the violently realised vision of Ewan's ghost returning home, is a wholly credible projection of the widow's desire to find closure in the form of redemption for her husband. Chris's final vision of Ewan's war-ravaged form is a classic moment of release signifying her coming to terms psychologically and emotionally with his death, as well as injecting a supernatural frisson of powerful physicality to the climax of The Song. The final sentence of the chapter is unashamedly romantic; the most significant relationship of Chris's young life comes to a heart-rending close as Ewan's shattered image staggers towards her: '*Oh lassie, I've come home!* he said, and went into the heart that was his forever' (SS244, italics in original text).

Mitchell had knowingly placed his new novel within the Scottish tradition through the abstruse intertextual reference attributed to the Reverend Gibbon in the Prelude to the poles of past literary representations of Scottish rustic life, from the sentimentalised picture of the kailyard novelists to the calculatedly miserablist riposte of *The House with the Green Shutters*. Yet in the narrator's abrupt trashing of the effete analogy of Gibbon's sardonically self-actualised minister, metafictionally the author of *Sunset Song* places his new fiction beyond the whole tradition, as an approach that's bold and fresh – and completely original. In the final analysis, the narrative of the first Gibbon novel testifies spontaneously and convincingly to lived experience, from the tiniest descriptive detailing of the land and the weather and the fields and the trees and the hills and the sharply etched observation of distinctive character foibles to the broader canvas, of the demise of a community, of the inexorable advance of civilisation, of the enduring sanctity of the natural world.

Sunset Song works so well on so many levels, all rolled into the one compelling narrative. At heart, Chris's story is a romance, but the book slips with comparable ease into the categories of intergenerational family saga, of rural realism, of Scottish epic, of more politically orientated forms like socialist realism, feminist fiction, anti-war protest, post-colonial revisionism and, most convincingly of all, of ecofiction. Chris's sensuous immersion in, and apprehension of, what she designates 'the sweetness of the Scottish land and skies' (*SS*42), allied with the author's channelling of a Proustian power of sensory recall, sets in motion a compelling train of thought that's crowned in the final pages of the trilogy, a theme that chimes perfectly with the contemporary interest in ecopolitics, promoting green values vouchsafing humanity's responsibilities for preserving the world round about us and affirming the physical and emotional well-being to be gleaned from establishing this harmonious relationship.

The roll call of Scottish literary greats would be immeasurably poorer without the names of James Leslie Mitchell and Lewis Grassic Gibbon in its ranks. And yet to define Mitchell as a great Scottish writer belittles his achievement. Having been catapulted to the forefront of the Scottish literary revival with the sensational success of *Sunset Song*, Mitchell came to terms with this new cultural realm with commendable speed. Within weeks the popularity that he had earned at large in Scotland, England and, later, in the United States had been replicated in literary circles; in addition to CM Grieve, Helen Cruickshank and James Barke became firm friends through their discovery of the first Gibbon novel and his address book expanded to include the contact details of a web of the most prominent Scottish writers of the day – George Blake, 'James Bridie', Neil Gunn, Compton Mackenzie, Edwin and Willa Muir, George Malcolm Thomson, Donald and Catherine Carswell. The new persona also opened up exciting new publishing opportunities, for fiction and non-fiction, for book reviews, for feature articles in Scottish journals and newspapers, and for spin-offs, such as, latterly, editorship of the Voice of Scotland series of Scottish monographs. However, Mitchell remained circumspect about the political ramifications of the resurgence of interest in Scottish affairs. The Scottish National Party was formally established virtually contemporaneously in 1934, but the expansion of the racial supremacism and cultural isolationism of right-wing nationalist politics throughout Europe prevented him from freely embracing his national culture. His most positive definition of his artistic position, in an article published in *The Free Man* in 1934, is guarded, as he talks of himself being 'non-Nationalist, and yet interested in this new revival of cultural and political Nationalism'.[12] He appeared even more wary when, clearly fearful of the advance of Nazism, he wrote to Neil Gunn just three months before the end of his life:

> I'm not really anti-Nationalist. But I loathe Fascism, and all the other dirty things that hide under the name. I doubt if you can ever have Nationalism without Communism.[13]

CLOUD HOWE

Scotland has a strong tradition in the novel of the small town, and Mitchell was very much aware that he was following on from previous fiction of this kind, most prominently as written by kailyard romanticists such as 'Ian Maclaren', author of *Beside the Bonnie Brier Bush,* already reviled in *Sunset Song*, JM Barrie and George Douglas Brown, whose dark counterblast to debased kailyard sentimentality *The House with the Green Shutters* again earns a sardonic citation in the previous volume. Initially, therefore, *Cloud Howe* can be viewed as rural realism in the traditional mould, with Mitchell's burgh of Segget carrying on directly from Maclaren's Drumtochty, Barrie's Thrums and Douglas Brown's Barbie – but of course Mitchell puts his own highly original spin on the form.

Mitchell's surviving notebook charts the evolution of his punctilious working plans for the new novel that fed in to the efficient production of the final typescript.[14] His preliminary pencil jottings even allow the reader to trace his actual thought process as he mulled over possibilities for the name of his new village before arriving at the final choice of Segget, triumphantly repeated and emphatically underlined following the rejection of a string of weaker alternatives: Drumnagatt, Culders, Culdyce, Drumnaders, Catcraig, Meiklebogs and Mondynes. This preparatory brainstorming also involved the creation of a detailed pencil map that, as was the case previously with *Sunset Song*, Jarrolds used as the basis of the inviting illustration reproduced on the book's endpapers. Both the initial listing of possible surnames alongside the sketch map and the fuller 'List of Characters' are notable for the absence of the Cronins – and indeed the random inventory of plot elements at this stage limits reference to the jute mill to its mendacious owners, in complete disregard of the spinners themselves who individually and collectively are responsible for adding a new urgent political dimension to the novel. Otherwise, the cast is pretty much intact, with the inevitable pruning of various dispensable village functionaries. Key scenes from the published novel are evident in this cataloguing of provisional set pieces sweeping up likely characters, anecdotes, vignettes, repartee, odd sayings and doggerel: the disrupted Armistice Day service, Chris's mournful memory of Ewan, the harrowing scene of the Kindnesses' destitution and rejection by Segget society, Robert Colquohoun's political idealism and disillusionment, Mowat's efforts to dupe the bank representative and the cruel death of Meiklebogs's horse. From here the author moves on smoothly to a numbered sequencing of the plot as a whole, lacking the opening section, including snatches of the inimitable Grassic Gibbon narrative style. The full typed draft was the relatively straightforward culmination of the diligent spadework done according to this well-honed creative practice.

As the intermediate volume in the trilogy, *Cloud Howe* in fact proved a blessing and a curse – exactly as Mitchell implied in casting it as a narrative bridge looking ahead to 'the blatant communism of Grey Granite'.[15] On the positive side, he was consolidating a phenomenally successful brand launched the year before with *Sunset Song*; on the negative side, though, not only had the first volume set an impossibly high standard of sheer narrative verve but it had thrown up a host of readers bowled over by a stylistic originality that they were eager to see reproducing the preternatural thrill of excitement that they had felt the first time round.

Mitchell's schema did just about all it could to stay true to the first novel's virtues. The title and chapter headings have a natural ambiance, metaphorically reflecting the darkening course of the narrative; the novel covers roughly the same timespan – where *Sunset Song* begins just before 1911 and goes up to 1919, in her final reflection in Nimbus Chris looks back on 'those ten full years' (*CH*158); and it's recognisably constructed according to the same climactic pattern in four extended flashback chapters, each framed by Chris's contemporary reflections, all preceded by a historical prologue. *Cloud Howe* trades directly on the success of *Sunset Song*, and much of the rustic vitality of Kinraddie carries over to Segget, summoning up the same naturalistic literary techniques: the narrative authenticity (employing the personas of Else Queen and young Ewan in addition to Chris herself); the anecdotal vibrancy of the plot, featuring outrageously unreliable narrators and jumping between the comic, the dramatic and the poignant; and earthy characterisation introducing in the first two chapters an equivalent cross-section of worthies, many of whom assume identical roles – Ake Ogilvie is the new Long Rob, Rob Moultrie a more severely political Chae Strachan, Alec Hogg the holier-than-thou successor of po-faced Gordon and Ellison, and Ag Moultrie is the new Mistress Munro, the malicious slanderer of character. Gibbon plants a similar clue to his realist approach with his secondary characterisation early on in Cumulus again through Chris, when she reflects on people's contrariness and tells Robert, *'they [folk] gossip and claik and are good and bad, and both together, mixed up and down'* (*CH*45, italics in original text). This wrongfooting tendency within the moral representation of his dramatis personae is diametrically opposed to Balzac's famous mission statement in his 'Avant-propos' to *La Comedie Humaine* in which he states his strategic aim to sort his characterisation into abstract types, in the mould of a social anthropologist classifying human species.[16] Taken as a whole, though, the indigenous half of the Segget population is in fact as frustratingly fickle in its political outlook as the Kinraddie crofters proved in the first book. Their thrawnness makes individuals like old Rob Moultrie, Dite Peat and old Leslie appear increasingly vulnerable as the novel progresses, again casting aspersions on the survival prospects of the whole social group that they represent. Yet where Robert pins his hopes for improving the world of the future on the spinners and on the nationwide possibilities of the General Strike, Chris remains pointedly detached, her dream of finding 'a third way to Life, unguessed, unhailed, never dreamed of yet' (CH144) setting up the search to be pursued by her in the third volume of the trilogy.

Continuity obviously is established principally with Chris's centrality as protagonist, with her new role as minister's wife placing her in an invidious social position within the community while underscoring her fiercely independent pursuit of her own values and principles, still socially and philosophically centred on the countryside in direct contrast with the nebulous cause of her husband's pastoral evangelism. Robert's gentle gregariousness and young Ewan's boyhood hyperactivity (drawing on the author's own adolescent spirit of adventure) are welcome additions to a storyline endowed with a lighter sprinkling of levity than its predecessor. The most striking innovation, though, is the work's overtly political character revolving around the interlinked tragedies of the local failure of Robert Colquohoun's Christian mission and the national failure of the General Strike. As ever, there's an acerbic physicality to Mitchell's descriptions of scenes of suffering and distress – the intensifying social squalor experienced by the spinners in the Segget wynds, Else's sexual abuse by Dalziel of the Meiklebogs (a shockingly blunt exposé of an ingrained form of malpractice latent within traditional farming circles), Chris's dramatic miscarriage symbolising the premature ending of the strike, the appalling report of the Kindness family's privations, forced in their homelessness to seek shelter in a pigsty where their baby has its thumb gnawed off by a rat (gleaned by Mitchell from a contemporary newspaper), the death of Robert, heartbroken and disillusioned at the book's finale.

Although the satire is less pointed, the Proem directly follows the pattern of the farcical portrait of the earlier Prelude, tracing what Chris in Cumulus dubs 'the pageant of history' made up of 'the clownings and cruelties of leaders and chiefs' (CH107). The Proem races from the mists of prehistory up through the hard-nosed opportunism of Hew Monte Alto's power grab to a similar curt dismissal of the modern descendants of the ruling Mowat dynasty, of whom the rustic narrator takes gruff delight in observing, 'and they lived and they died and they went to their place' (*CH*6). The Proem performs an identical function to the Prelude earlier, providing an ironic historical backdrop for the action to come, concentrating largely on ridiculing the iniquities of the 'gentry' and turning the traditional social and literary ethos on its head by bringing the 'common' sector into the foreground. This time round, though, the spinners emerge as the much more hardened subaltern element set against the entitled elite in the author's introductory mélange of legend, history and pure invention. Significantly, later, in Stratus, Ewan echoes his mother's distrust of conventional history, commenting, 'most of the histories were dull as ditchwater, with their kings and their battles and their dates and such muck, you wondered how the people had lived in those times' (*CH*118–9). This prepares him for his low-key political role in the book, his disarming ingenuousness and friendship with Charlie Cronin making him the main vehicle for social comment on the impoverished conditions that the spinners live in.

The passage of time is established at the start of the second book through Chris's quiet reflection on the changes that have overtaken her former homeland of Kinraddie: the sound of tractors working the fields provides a mechanised soundtrack while the livestock has now principally turned to sheep, leaving her feeling lost in 'the land so strange', so that 'she half-longed to be gone' (*CH*13). Within the tripartite framework of the trilogy *Cloud Howe* required a social setting that fell in between country and city, with the town of Segget fitting the bill admirably, defined by Robert in advance as 'something betwixt and between' (*CH*21). While Leslie Mitchell had personal experience of living in two country parishes and two Scottish cities, it stands to reason that he would fill the gap in his knowledge for the intermediate setting by drawing on the closest small town of his acquaintance – Inverbervie, lying less than five miles down the road from Bloomfield towards the sea.

While the burgh of Inverbervie itself is name-checked regularly in *Cloud Howe*, and indeed throughout the trilogy (under its original twelfth-century name of Bervie), the Royal Toun next to Mitchell's home parish of Arbuthnott contributed most significantly to the fictional setting of Segget, whose name cast even further back to the author's place of birth at Auchterless. The final two pages of the Proem paint a picture of a typical modern industrial town that experienced an economic revival with the arrival of two jute mills along with the railway, but with the spinners actually being described as an imported workforce from Bervie, subsequently splitting the town into two autonomous districts, the East Wynd, or New Toun, and the West Wynd, or Old Toun. The general similarities with Inverbervie are notable, despite Mitchell's relocation of Segget inland from the coast; the modern industrial history of Inverbervie directly parallels Segget's, with Mitchell carrying the social profile of the burgh as it developed from the first decades of the twentieth century forward to the most acute socio-political convulsion of the 1920s surrounding the General Strike and the onset of the Great Depression. The political militancy of the intermediate novel in the trilogy holds out some promise, but the ineffectuality of the formal Labour movement at the time proves conclusive, allowing the political status quo to persist, with the apathetic bourgeoisie, the established authorities and the industrial oligarchs regaining an even firmer stranglehold over the health and prosperity of the people. Wholesale disillusionment with the mainstream parties empowers extremist minorities such as the fascists (conflated with nationalists) and gives rise to unprincipled and unworkable coalition politics – a sorry pattern to be repeated in Britain up to recent times. The failure of the political left is epitomised by the career of Ramsay MacDonald, denounced in Segget by those in the know and later demonised as 'The Wrecker' by Mitchell in the Gibbon essay of that name in *Scottish Scene* for his moderate Labour Government of 1929 to 1931 and for his subsequent alliance in a marriage of convenience with the Conservatives in the National Government from 1931.

The author trims the contemporary population of Bervie for his own fictive purposes, reducing Segget to 'less than a thousand souls' (*CH*24) split roughly between the indigenous population and the spinners, thereby creating a more manageable canvas for his characterisation. The extended family of the Cronins is his principal vehicle for social commentary throughout *Cloud Howe*, representing the overcrowding and deprivation that were concomitants of the rapid development of the flax and jute industries in the area, with the additional impact of the insidious Means Test being traced towards the novel's close (*CH*198–9). Despite young Charlie Cronin's defiant affirmation to Ewan of the spinners' individual identity – 'he said the folk in New Toun were daft to speak of the folk in the Mills as only spinners, there were foremen and weavers, and a lot more besides' (*CH*117) – the author paints the mills and the spinners with a broad brush, glossing over the conditions that historically were peculiar to the circumstances of this particular workforce: the local preference for flax rather than jute, the heavy reliance on female labour (which was cheap as well as dextrous) or the occupational hazard for employees of permanent deafness caused by the incessant clattering of the machinery. Perhaps pressure of time, as ever, caught up with him, or maybe he simply sacrificed the detail in order to emphasise the plight of the subaltern classes in general.

Just like its predecessor, the characterisation of *Cloud Howe* incorporates extensive borrowings stockpiled by Mitchell from real life and especially from the contemporary population of Inverbervie. Dominie Geddes and his wife, Will Melvin the hotelier, MacDougall Brown the Segget grocer, Sim Leslie ('Feet') the bobby and local mill magnate Alex Mowat anecdotally all had their origins in everyday Bervie. In addition, Mitchell expropriated the splendid farm name of Meiklebogs from his distant past in Auchterless, imported the angelic war memorial in Segget from Montrose and even included for good measure a thumbnail sketch of his old home on the Reisk back at Arbuthnott (*CH*172–3).

The discrete roles assumed by Chris and Ewan later in *Grey Granite* are flagged up in *Cloud Howe*. While she remains emotionally engaged with issues in past and present relating to social injustice, politically Chris remains apart. Her main calling is a more profound one, enmeshed with the natural world, and as ever, her animus is most alive to the beauties around her, calling into play some of the author's most spontaneous descriptive work. Meanwhile, Chris gives Ewan her personal seal of approval, her endorsement extending way beyond mere maternal pride as she recognises him as 'one of the few who might save the times, watching the Ice and the winter come, unflustered, unfrightened, with quiet, cold eyes' (*CH*197). His cool rationalism, crucially, is shown to be humanised by his involvement with the Cronins and by his experience of the poverty of the spinners as a whole, which leaves him towards the end of the novel 'turning to look in the face of Life' (*CH*200). Ewan's bildungsroman thus straddles *Cloud Howe* and *Grey Granite*, forging one of the main connective links.

As with *Sunset Song*, however, the political impact of the book rests with the climax, and indeed the parallelism of the endings of these first two novels is highly instructive. Robert's sermon in *Cloud Howe* again provides a summary of the social commentary attenuated throughout the book, building up to the urgent call for a militant political solution to alleviate the appalling poverty experienced by the proletariat; Robert's own search for salvation in Christian socialism has proved hopelessly, tragically ineffective, pointing the way forward to the radicalism of the next volume. His personal disillusionment bolsters the political message of his sermon, as he rouses himself at the end to conclude:

> *There is no hope for the world at all – as I, the least of His followers see – except it forget the dream of the Christ, forget the creeds that they forged in His shadow when their primal faith in the God was loosed – and turn and seek with unclouded eyes, not that sad vision that leaves hunger unfed, the wail of children in unending dark, the cry of human flesh eaten by beasts ... . But a stark, sure creed that will cut like a knife, a surgeon's knife through the doubt and disease – men with unclouded eyes may yet find it, and far off yet in the times to be, on an earth at peace, living and joyous, the Christ come back –* (*CH*210–11, italics in original text)

The political theme promoting a substantive shift from reformist to revolutionary politics invoking an unforgivingly clinical response to the contemporary social malaise is all the more convincing for the directness of its presentation, realistically couched in a social context that reflects the widespread ignorance and cynicism of the locals with regard to political matters. There is absolutely no dilution or romanticisation of the political task ahead. The author drew directly upon the bright socialist ethics of his own early adulthood in his representation of Robert's idealism; his death is a full and final renunciation of this credo, as a left-wing response that has now become totally outmoded.

GREY GRANITE

Grey Granite moves right away from the past to a time setting that's burningly topical. The book's dedication to Hugh MacDiarmid, by then a public figure inviting lionisation and demonisation across the United Kingdom in equal measure, flags up the challenging political character of the volume while the title, referencing what the author termed in his essay on Aberdeen 'one of the most enduring and indestructible and appalling building-materials in use on our planet' (*Sm*111), immediately jars with the extended cloud metaphor of the preceding volume. The chapter titles Epidote, Sphene, Apatite and Zircon are taken elliptically from types of granitic rocks, and the author's unexplained references to these minerals again suggests a new abstruse mode of approach. However, a welcome coherence is recreated with the novel's familiar quartering into four bulky chapters, as ever framed by Chris's controlling focalisation.

Mitchell's original adaptation of the Bartholomew Map of Kincardineshire places his fictional city of Dundon (later rechristened Duncairn) on the North Sea coast as the southernmost of the three locations for the trilogy, located just a mile to the north of Kinneff and introduced in the opening of the novel as twenty miles away from Segget (*GG*4). The author's prefatory disclaimer in his 'Cautionary Note', that Duncairn is 'merely the city which the inhabitants of the Mearns (not foreseeing my requirements in completing my trilogy) have hitherto failed to build' (*GG*viii), demands to be taken at face value, although the supposedly imaginary setting boasts components of names and topography drawn from different locations in Scotland – particularly Aberdeen and Edinburgh. While an incomplete typescript for a 'Curtain Raiser' for the urban novel languishes in Mitchell's papers,[17] he rejected this introductory preamble as something that had become a formulaic and cumbersome distraction from the insistent modernity of his contemporary city. Turning his eye for detail to the cityscape, Mitchell plunges the reader without ceremony straight into Chris's new situation at Ma Cleghorn's guesthouse. The concentrated unnaturalness of the surroundings recalls the stylisation of the exemplary novels of socialist realism, such as Gorky's *Mother* (1906) and Gladkov's

Cement (1925) – both of which Mitchell owned – which in fact had been embraced as part of the programmatic approach to state-sanctioned literature newly adopted at the Soviet Writers' Congress held in Moscow in August of 1934 and that were influential on the Scottish author's politicised aesthetic.[18] Despite Mitchell's own trepidation about using an urban setting, the sheer vibrancy of the city scene repeatedly calls his energetic descriptive powers into play, with his diction now consciously modernised to include harsh slang (even up to the strident profanity of 'bastard' creeping into the dialogue) as well as frequent scientific allusions – to iron, steel, celluloid – and with the literal representation of the heavy engineering work carried out within Gowans and Gloag's setting a convincing impression of rampant industrialism right at the social heart of the book.

Duncairn is a totally different kind of setting from Kinraddie and even Segget, a fractured locale reflecting a quite different authorial purpose, to broaden the accessibility of the emergent social and political messages by establishing the representative status of his modern city. Covering a period of just thirty months, the timescale of *Grey Granite* is noticeably more compressed than the earlier volumes, bringing the whole project bang up to date with affairs in 1934. This time constraint gives licence for a more expansive and informed appreciation of the social setting very much in keeping with the author's political aims, while the action appears more packed and frenetic. Consequently, the narrative of the third novel of the trilogy is much less free-flowing than its predecessors', with the notable exceptions of the rural set-pieces of the sojourn by Chris, Ewan and Ellen out to Echt in Epidote and the outings by Ewan and Ellen to Drumtochty in Apatite and Zircon, calm interstices that serve to underline the archaic reality of Chris's country roots.

In 'Literary Lights' in 1934 Mitchell in fact had already openly expressed his misgivings about his ability to conjure up techniques adequate to cope with the broad canvas of the Scottish city:

> His scene so far has been a comparatively uncrowded and simple one – the countryside and village of modern Scotland. Whether his technique is adequate to compass and express the life of an industrialized Scots town in all its complexity is yet to be

demonstrated; whether his peculiar style may not become either intolerably mannered or degenerate, in the fashion of Joyce, into the unfortunate unintelligibilities of a literary second childhood, is also in question. (*Sm*135)

Most pressingly, Mitchell was facing the problem of characterisation painted on an infinitely broader scale, a problem that he solved ingeniously by supplementing conventional individualisation (for example, of Ewan's workmates Alick Watson, Norman Cruickshank and Geordie Bruce) with a scattergun spraying of workers' Christian names multiplying the workers' experiences: Will, Peter, Tam, Andrew, Charlie, Leslie, Thomas, Neil, Jim, Sam, Rob, Ian, Malcolm. The refrains of the increasingly desperate workers are ironically counterpointed with recurring montages relaying soundbites denoting the intransigence of archetypes coming from more affluent and powerful conglomerates, from the lower-middle-class professionals gathered in Ma Cleghorn's guest house to the establishment figures and civic dignitaries of Duncairn openly flouting their social responsibilities: a journalist, the minister, a Labour councillor, the Chief of Police and the Lord Provost.

Grey Granite is in fact very much a novel of strategic contrasts, in structure and characterisation, and in ideology. As twin protagonists, the paths of Chris and Ewan are double tracked to personify the two most prominent approaches to life disentangled from the author's own makeup – broadly, the philosophical and the political. In the foreground of the novel the fortunes of Chris and Ewan unfold in parallel, with Chris, ever constant in her peasant individuality, gradually pulling away from society towards her final existential destiny, 'concerning none and concerned with none' (*GG*203), alone and independent, coming full circle in the most fitting ending of the book welcoming her death at her birthplace, the croft of Cairndhu back at Echt. Ewan by contrast is won away from his independent self and drawn towards his political mission, a modern Spartacus sacrificing his personal destiny to the people's cause. Both responses are run together and built up as alternative, valid, approaches to life in a world governed by the overarching principle of change. Ewan aims to make sense of the historical process, to gain control over the factors that shape society and that in the past – as in *Sunset*

Song and *Cloud Howe* – have had tragic political consequences. He wishes to gain political control in order to govern the future, to change it for the better. However, the whole historical plane is subsumed within the cyclical pattern of reality that Chris is bound up in, where change is continuous but repetitive. This cycle is epitomised in nature, or the Land, in the organic norm of birth, growth, death and, crucially, renewal, and in the constant revolution of the seasons. Ultimately, then, Chris's experience has a spiritual or religious character in that it represents the search beyond human existence for stability and permanence.

The process by which eighteen-year-old Ewan is won away from his cerebral intellectualism to a warmer interest in the welfare of humankind harks back to Mitchell's character-forming experiences as a young man in Aberdeen and Glasgow. More obviously, Chris is still very much fashioned in her creator's image in her search for a modern philosophy that represents her sublime engagement with the natural world. These twin impulses are the central responses to life succinctly summed up by Ewan in his 'Last Supper' with Chris in the penultimate scene of the book as the urgently capitalised choice between 'FREEDOM and GOD' (*GG*202).

Structurally *Grey Granite* is superbly integrated. The expository chapter, Epidote, introduces a new world that's crowded, frantic, mechanised and fragmented. Significantly, Ewan's securing of a four-year apprenticeship at Gowans and Gloag's steelworks is the motivation behind their move, and Mitchell's impression of Ewan's work and of his industrial workplace is convincingly detailed, again strongly redolent of the bold socialist realist images of the heroic workman paraded in Soviet iconography at the time. The chronically deprived conditions that the workers live in is flagged up in the generic vignette of the humdrum life of a typically poor family trapped in a Paldy Parish tenement denied all prospect of finding secure employment and deprived of political hope. Ewan's workmates and Chris's maid Meg Watson become the principal means for Mitchell to expose the poverty endemically afflicting the urban poor, whose political disenchantment with the supine mainstream parties appears eminently understandable.

As the novel progresses, the sense of social fragmentation steadily discloses a series of contrasts and tensions: between past and present, and present and future; country and city; employed and unemployed; workforce and management; proletariat and bourgeoisie; reformist gradualism and revolutionary militancy; left-wing and right-wing ideologies (graduating into the central opposition between communism and fascism). Set against the manifold confusion of the world, though, the political options appear severely limited, with Douglasism being denounced as an equally poor successor to the effete Labour politics of Ramsay MacDonald and with the Young League promoted by Ewan and Ellen emerging as an insipid response to the harshness of the times. The increasingly insidious effects of the Means Test administered by the unsympathetic PAC (Public Assistance Committee) inevitably drives Ewan towards wily campaigner Jim Trease and his revolutionary Communist Party as the sole radical alternative capable of mounting a challenge to the political stagnation of 1934, with strikes and industrial action, public demonstrations and the nationwide protest of the hunger marches, most recently orchestrated in real life in January and February of 1934, indicating the hard-line measures called for in order to make proper inroads to the prevailing Scottish and British realpolitik.[19]

Mitchell had been actively involved with revolutionary politics from his teens, and while there's compelling evidence that he was welcomed into a series of radical political groups throughout his life, he was never a card-carrying member of the Communist Party of Great Britain (CPGB) – most probably out of professional discretion. Towards the end of his life, however, he joined the British section of Writers' International, which offered the perfect home for someone with his ideological profile as a free-thinking left-wing writer of what is best defined by French Marxist Louis Aragon, himself a sprightly contributor to their in-house journal *Left Review*, as 'littérature engagée'.[20] With civil unrest growing throughout the 1930s, publishers responded to the gathering interest shown by novelists from all over Britain in tackling social and political issues, with a plethora of titles such as Walter Greenwood's *Love on the Dole* (1933), Dot Allan's *Hunger March* (1934), Walter Brierley's *Means-Test Man* (1935) and Lewis Jones's *Cwmardy* (1937), all in their own right fine examples of the campaigning novel, adding to the early example shown by Lewis Grassic Gibbon and James Barke in Scotland. The influential journal *Left*

Review formed by the British section of Writers' International (more combatively christened Revolutionary Writers of the World) singlehandedly legitimised this politicisation of art and culture, and where formerly left-wing writers were stigmatised by formal association with the CPGB, now engagement in radical politics by those later gathered under the collective heading of 'the Auden Generation' became almost a mark of distinction for artists and writers.[21] Mitchell had always grappled with social and political concerns in his writing, and now his assured response to the Writers' International debate placed him in the vanguard of the movement.

Left Review was a uniquely open forum for artists interested in exploring the relationship between culture and politics, embracing everything from hard-left agitprop to the more liberal espousal of democratic values all united within the steadily evolving popular front under an anti-fascist banner. The journal's opening debate centred on the Writers' International 'Controversy' begun in the third number in December 1934, and the conversation carried on with tremendous fervour through the following three editions. The fundamental issues at stake were all dear to Mitchell's heart, focusing on the general nature of literature, on the relationship between literature and society and, most invigoratingly, on the political duty of the writer. The Grassic Gibbon contribution is forthright and clear-sighted, first of all denouncing the 'bolshevik blah' of party line writers who couch prescriptive criticism in 'bad Marxian patter', whose literary judgement is thought to be compromised by their political rigidity and who, falling prey to 'wish-fulfilment dreams', harbour an unrealistic sense of the declining influence of capitalist literature. Untrammelled by received party dogma, Mitchell goes on to elucidate his own viewpoint. Ultimately this passionate communiqué represents his lasting manifesto as a political writer and the theoretical fulfilment of his lifetime's quest to find a literary identity fusing his artistic and political ideals.

Having cleared the way with forceful swipes at his less enlightened colleagues, Mitchell carries on to ally himself with the cause, proclaiming unequivocally, 'I am a revolutionary writer' and observing: 'having said all this in criticism, I'll proceed to a little construction'. His letter closes with a rallying cry proposing a practical tick list for 'a union of revolutionary writers' that he envisages constituting 'a shock-brigade'. His concluding remarks are unequivocal in defining how he views his own literary role in past and present, absolutely dedicated to a common political end and yet unwilling to suspend his own political judgement:

> I hate capitalism; all my books are explicit or implicit propaganda. But because I'm a revolutionist I see no reason for gainsaying my own critical judgment – hence this letter! (*Sm*739)

Mitchell refrained from overplaying his hand in the endorsement of CP politics in *Grey Granite*, freely dramatising the obstacles facing the effective fulfilment of the party's objectives, from the reactionary opposition mobilised among the political establishment and the democratically elected authorities to the unpredictability, contrariness and sheer obdurate apathy of the people whose cause they are representing, as well as the endless internecine squabbling among its own members. The final outlook for their political future, as articulated by the CP veteran Jim Trease, is pragmatic and down to earth, reflecting the author's own unromanticised standpoint – and indeed accurately casting ahead to the catastrophic events that were to shake the world for the remainder of the century:

> He said he misdoubted they'd ever see workers' revolution in their time, capitalism had taken crises before and would take them again, it was well enough organized in Great Britain to carry ten million unemployed let alone the two and a half of to-day, Fascism would stabilize and wars help, they were coming, the wars, but coming slow. (*GG*181)

In comparison with the rustic simplicities of Kinraddie, then, the city of Duncairn appears infinitely more complex and much, much more menacing. Quite rightly, the author shows that life in modern Scotland yields very few pat answers – although despite misguided criticism of the novel from the 1960s onwards that sought to downplay Ewan's role in the novel, Ewan the doctrinaire CP activist is recognised as the author's bluntly direct and resolute political mouthpiece.

One of the key scenes in *Grey Granite* concerns the high-water mark in Ewan's political development, his humanitarian afflatus in the Museum Galleries in Duncairn that passionately promotes the claims of the ordinary people underpinning the militant political action in the book, and in Britain in the 1930s. Alongside this, a curiously anomalous and discordant view of art, culture and media forms a running theme in the novel, comprehensively denouncing the radio, the press (both the tabloid *Runner* and the broadsheet *Tory Pictman*), the cinema and the visual arts, as well as literature (with James Pittendrigh MacGillivray, Marion Angus, Lewis Spence and even Hugh MacDiarmid, as 'Hugo MacDownall', all taking hits [GG31]). In accordance with Mitchell's hardening politics, aesthetic appeal was counting for less and less, and art denuded of socio-political purpose was now deemed to be worthless. In the Museum Gallery in Sphene Ewan receives a 'flaring savage sickness', a familiar Spartacus-like vision of the sufferings experienced by the ordinary people throughout history, interestingly commending Spartacus and the Spartacists, together with the Haitian Toussaint Louverture, the mastermind behind the only recorded successful slave insurrection ever staged (GG72–3). Ewan updates the picture to include more urgently appealing groups, 'the men of your kin, peasants and slaves and common folk and their ghastly lives through six thousand years', and his response to the unidentified socially skewed old master preserved from the Italian Renaissance, featuring 'soldiers, a cardinal, an angel or so, and a throng of keelies cheering like hell about nothing at all – in the background, as usual', indirectly defines the author's own purpose, to bring working-class life into the foreground and to redress the political balance in his art in favour of the subaltern classes whose cause traditionally has been neglected. This refrain is reprised in Apatite with arresting topicality when the social and political polarisation of the world is brought right up to date, as Ewan receives a 'stinging bliss' of understanding following his brutalisation by the police as a Communist agitator, becoming representative himself of all modern-day sufferings, and indeed a universal symbol of repressed peoples:

> [...] lost and be-bloodied in a hundred broken and tortured bodies all over the world, in Scotland, in England, in the torture-dens of the Nazis in Germany, in the torment-pits of the Polish Ukraine, a

livid, twisted thing in the prisons where they tortured the Nanking Communists, a Negro boy in an Alabama cell while they thrust the razors into his flesh, castrating with a lingering cruelty and care. He was one with them all, a long wail of sobbing mouths and wrung flesh, tortured and tormented by the world's Masters while those Masters lied about Progress through Peace, Democracy, Justice, the Heritage of Culture – even as they'd lied in the days of Spartacus, lying now through their hacks in pulpit and press, in the slobberings of middle-class pacifists, the tawdry promisings of Labourites, Douglasites … . And a kind of stinging bliss came upon him, knowledge that he was that army itself – that army of pain and blood and torment that was yet but the raggedest van of the hordes of the Last of the Classes, the Ancient Lowly, trampling the ways behind it unstayable: up and up, a dark sea of faces, banners red in the blood from the prisons, torn entrails of tortured workers their banners, the enslavement and oppression of six thousand years a cry and a singing that echoed to the stars. No retreat, no safety, no escape for them, no reward, thrust up by the black, blind tide to take the first brunt of impact, first glory, first death, first life as it never yet had been lived – (*GG*137)

Grey Granite captures the zeitgeist of the 1930s with vigour and imagination, and even the musical refrains of 'The Internationale' and 'The Red Flag' (more fleetingly cited previously in *Stained Radiance*) tie it down to a specific time frame when working-class politics appeared to be coming to a militant crescendo. And, indeed, the underlying principles of the book remain universally relevant, socially, politically and philosophically. Mitchell's fundamental socio-political critique has a particularly strong resonance in Europe in the twenty-first century, when neoliberal capitalism embracing the principles of austerity and private enterprise still manifestly serves the interests of the entitled minority.

Although Chris is not the political hero in any of the component novels and despite the fact that the diffuse characterisation makes *Grey Granite* more of an ensemble piece than its predecessors, she dominates the trilogy, and Gibbon fully exploits her as the central figure. A free spirit, her experience is authoritative and definitive: she not only articulates the clearest existential philosophy; she embodies and enacts it. Like Ewan, Chris resists all the romanticised belief systems in search of a faith of empirical conviction, and their divergent responses both capitalise on the trilogy's constant refrain affirming the spiritual emptiness of life. However, where Ewan finds his fulfilment in the secular ideology of Marxist–Leninism, Chris follows a very different path. She may be detached in terms of formal political allegiance, but she isn't entirely passive politically; as the definitive peasant, her sympathies lie throughout with the ordinary people at the grass roots, especially when she considers Scotland's inglorious past. Over and above this, amidst the vast panoply of ideas circulating in the trilogy as a whole, in her matter-of-fact approach to life and death Chris provides the bedrock for the most profound themes of the trilogy. The trilogy's structure in fact emphasises the climactic import of her final valediction, her longed-for spiritual fulfilment, as the volume's endgame has a decisive air of finality that has been well prepared for, and that stands in pointed contrast with the indeterminate conclusions of both *Sunset Song* and *Cloud Howe*. As she is the work's lynchpin, Chris's end is final and complete.

Marxist theory has a strong hold on the book's political theme, and it spills over into the more profound areas of the volume in the form of the scientific rationalism espoused by Ewan and by Ellen Johns. Chris's own standpoint echoes their unsentimental objectivity, apprehending life and death in stolidly physical, non-spiritual terms as she reaches back to emphasise the finality of the losses adumbrated of everyone who had touched her past: her father, her mother, the twins, Ewan, Long Rob, Robert. This materialism has a bleakness that extends throughout Mitchell's work, the stripping down of life to the bare essentials of a spiritually barren universe devoid of ulterior meaning anticipating mainstream developments in European thinking that evolved after the First World War, pre-eminently existentialism and absurdism. This marks the trilogy out as a thoroughly modern book, associating the author with writers from Kafka and Sartre to Camus and Beckett who have made high art of the belief in the inherent hopelessness and incoherence of the human condition.

Chris's search for enlightenment was initiated in her musings at the standing stones in *Sunset Song*, yearning for understanding of her place in the world around her and nurtured by the instinctual love of nature that was fostered by her mother. This quest continued in *Cloud Howe*, in which she considered the possibility of 'a third way to Life' (*CH*144) involving a search for 'her surety unshaken' (*CH*173). Throughout the final novel Chris becomes more closely thirled to the aim of pursuing her own salvation. In Apatite she renounces the toil and strife of everyday life in Duncairn, consoling herself that her final destiny is entirely independent. In Zircon she finally asserts her full individuality and receives a salutary epiphany in return.

At the beginning of the section from her elevated vantage point at the top of the Barmekin – the exact spot where Mitchell himself scribbled down his ending – the author observes with disarming casualness how Chris 'looked down with untroubled eyes on the world below' (*GG*161), and a little later the sense of release that she achieves is presented as an integral part of the ritualistic process of self-discovery:

> That dreadful storm she'd once visioned stripping her bare was all about her, and she feared it no longer, eager to be naked, alone and unfriended, facing the last realities with a cool, clear wonder, an unhasting desire. (*GG*189)

By the final pages of the volume Chris is ready to embrace her personal destiny, as 'she had found the last road she wanted and taken it, concerning none and concerned with none' (*GG*203). There's a gentle serenity and dignity about Chris's death, represented with implicit metaphysicality as she loses consciousness, moving to a purely sensory functionality before finally she surrenders to the natural environment around her, following her dying apprehension of natural harmony:

> And that was the best deliverance of all, as she saw it now, sitting here quiet – that that Change who ruled the earth and the sky and the waters underneath the earth, Change whose face she'd once feared to see, whose right hand was Death and whose left hand Life, might be stayed by none of the dreams of men, love, hate, compassion, anger or pity, gods or devils or wild crying to the sky. He passed and repassed in the ways of the wind, Deliverer, Destroyer and Friend in one. (*GG*203)

Chris's calm acceptance of her fate is dramatic validation of this final vision. Insensate at the last, she is assimilated into the earth, absorbed by the organic base whose contrasting elements – Death and Life, Deliverer, Destroyer, Friend – are fused into the universal locus of Change. The natural elements of the rain and the passing lapwings inconspicuously representing the living quick continue after Chris gently slips away into oblivion.

Chris's narrative rightly brings Mitchell's epic to a triumphant close, signalling in exultant capitalisation 'THE END OF A SCOTS QUAIR', the lyrical immediacy of her gentle surrender to her 'fiere' of the Land at the end of the volume offering the reader a more moving and conclusive resolution than Ewan's subdued disappearance to the south on the selfless mission to further the revolutionary CP struggle. The atemporal vision of natural harmony bound up in the universal principle of Change gives Chris a sense of belonging, finally at peace with herself and with her surroundings. The descriptive power of the closing paragraphs subtly marrying the material with the ethereal and slipping at the climax from free indirect speech to impersonal third person narrative fully testifies to the spontaneous manner of the scene's composition, as Leslie Mitchell sat among the ancient stones within the iron age hillfort at the summit of the Barmekin hill:

> Lights had sprung up far in the hills, in little touns for a sunset minute while the folk tirred and went off to their beds, miles away, thin peeks in the summer dark.
> Time she went home herself.
> But she still sat on as one by one the lights went out and the rain came, beating the stones about her, and falling all that night while she still sat there, presently feeling no longer the touch of the rain or hearing the sound of the lapwings going by. (GG203-4)

A Scots Quair as a whole has set a bracing challenge over the years in the realm of gender politics that is only now being fully appreciated. This in fact is one of the main reasons for the trilogy's mixed reception in Mitchell's native Northeast. Chris Guthrie goes her own way, but by doing so she flies in the face of convention and flouts accepted norms, conducting herself in a manner that traditionally would be deemed transgressive: attending her father's funeral as principal mourner, marrying indecently swiftly after the death of her father, taking over the lease of Blawearie – a shockingly radical thing for the daughter to do, rather than selling up – participating in extra-marital sex with Long Rob in retaliation against her errant husband, and finally returning alone to work the croft of Cairndhu single-handedly. Her actions are backed up by her propensity for basically just speaking out on a whole assortment of matters that previously had lain largely unquestioned.

Chris is a true feminist icon within the pantheon of iconoclasts in Mitchell's fiction who embody the author's own desire to subject key ideas and rules and routines governing our behaviour to fearless scrutiny. Mitchell's proto-feminist sympathies, then, may be seen as one facet of his lifelong engagement with human rights as a whole, emerging from his awareness in the Northeast of the severely patriarchal character of a society in which the mother of the family was consigned to a thankless remit, with responsibilities chiefly revolving around looking after the home and caring for the children (with a raft of occasional add-ons including helping out with the farm work at busy pressure points of the year), and in which acknowledgement of the husband's dominant status and subservience to his will were absolutes.

In keeping with the bricolage steadfastly emerging from the slew of ideas pervading his literary oeuvre, the most profound ramifications of Mitchell's fiction as a whole may be seen in the positive rapport represented between the female protagonist and nature. The trilogy is pivoted on a female protagonist who wins free of the norms that are promulgated and passed down in male society; Chris has the independence of thought and openness to experience that enables her to feel and to describe the harmonious relationship that she comes to enjoy with the natural world at large. Her intimate understanding of the universal principle of change is an instinct that comes from her appreciation of the organic cycle of birth, life and death that as a female she is directly bound up with; her intellectual conception of her philosophical vision embodied in the agricultural year, finding classical validation in the writings of Heraclitus, appears both invigoratingly fresh and convincingly logical. When finally Mitchell charts her return alone to the landscape of Echt that had sustained her spiritually, her personal epiphany aligns her with the Romantic poets and the pantheistic veneration of nature of Wordsworth and Coleridge, and yet her whole fictive existence has a spiritual significance that is more convincingly female. As authorial avatar, her fate at the end of the trilogy acquires a profound thematic meaning representing the writer's own deepest held philosophical beliefs.

Chris's death significantly isn't portrayed in such final terms, as she's left at one with her 'fiere' of the Land while nature takes its course, a beautifully tranquil scene that crowns the thematic movement that has been mapped out across the volume as a whole articulating her growing apprehension of humankind's organic accommodation by nature at large.

SCOTTISH SCENE: OR THE INTELLIGENT MAN'S GUIDE TO ALBYN

Having struck gold and created a whole new avenue for his writing with *Sunset Song*, Mitchell set about promoting his new 'cousin' with great gusto. Letters were strategically fired off to the local press back in the Northeast, to national Scottish newspapers and to literary journals that flourished with the contemporary reawakening in Scottish cultural awareness. The Grassic Gibbon by-line became increasingly prominent, attached to occasional features and book reviews and muscling in on Mitchell's establish territory; a conventional Mitchell review of *The Diffusion of Culture* by Diffusionist guru Grafton Elliot Smith in the lively Scottish periodical *The Free Man* shared the same page with a lusty piece of Gibbon anti-kailyard invective, while his final volume *Nine Against the Unknown* diplomatically split the credits between Mitchell and Gibbon. The Grassic Gibbon gravy train was expanding profitably before he died; not only was he contemplating a whole raft of alternative Gibbon fiction books but he had found himself a prestigious post as editor for Routledge's The Voice of Scotland series of polemical volumes analysing key aspects of Scotland's culture and history.

Scottish Scene appeared among a swelling tide of fashionable 'state of the nation' volumes published about Scotland in the early 1930s.[22] It's a ragbag of a book recycling lesser pieces by both Gibbon and MacDiarmid padded out with brand new essays and contemporary newspaper clippings taken from the Scottish press. It's sprawling, uneven, impressionistic, opinionated and contradictory – which is precisely the point. There's no better text for opening a window on to the complexities of the Scottish political and cultural landscape in the years leading up to the Second World War.

The joint authors of this outspoken Scottish compendium were physically separated by the length of the British Isles, with Mitchell firmly ensconced in Welwyn Garden City and Grieve seeking sanctuary from his travails at the time in retreat to the remote Shetland isle of Whalsay. This meant that their contributions were written effectively without collaboration, producing a spiky sense of unpredictability and quite overwhelming heterogeneity. The project was Mitchell's original conception, and he was the creative fulcrum from his initial approach to Grieve right through to designing the amusingly cartoonish dustjacket. Mitchell's greater sense of ownership is reflected in the more consistent quality that's struck across his contributions.

The five Gibbon stories gathered in *Scottish Scene* collectively roll out the same narrative modes and techniques pioneered in the trilogy, with the author using the same flexible narrative approach throughout that marries the immediacy of first person and the omniscient scope of multiple viewpoints. The four rural stories are heavily anthologised offshoots from *Sunset Song* imbued with the same potent spirit of place and portraying the same heavily realised Mearns farming world. The fictional locations of Kinraddie and Segget appear by name, as do many of the familiar Mearns landmarks – the Bervie Water, Kinneff, Stonehive (Stonehaven), Mondynes, the Grampian Hills. The setting again lies at the very heart of the stories, as a force that governs human behaviour; all four works are steeped in the farming year, with the author's effortless Heaneyesque ability to elevate at a stroke seemingly prosaic and commonplace description to poetic heights very much in evidence. In addition, the prevalence of the anti-hero as protagonist throughout the series underlines the author's profound ambivalence about the human cost of the life of the land.

Employing the same infectious prose style and tapping in to Mitchell's farming roots in the Mearns, 'Greenden', the first of three Gibbon pieces originally published in *The Scots Magazine*, appeared in the December edition in 1932, just three months after *Sunset Song* burst on to the scene, as a reworking of a fairly orthodox Mitchell storyline titled 'The Lost Whaler' contained in précis form among his papers (*Sm*805). Mitchell had already racked up invaluable experience with the pared down form of the short story, expertly brought to bear on his latest work as a semi-realistic fable probing the mystical power that nature wields over the human realm and exploring the febrile relationship developing between female protagonist Ellen Simpson and the natural world round about. The rather laboured hymn motif of 'There is a Green Hill Far Away' underscores the tragic progress of the plot, climaxing in Ellen Simpson's suicide. 'Greenden' is absolutely unique among the Gibbon stories, as a gripping psychodrama tracing the implosion of a marriage that has the lasting impact of an eco-fable about the enigmatic power of the natural world. The style of the Scots story proves all-important to its appeal in harnessing the teasing *Polychromata*-style plot to vernacular reality. The theme of the sublime influence of the natural realm so beautifully captured in Chris Guthrie's wholesome relationship with the Land here has a negative twist, as Ellen the scorned wife affirms the hostile predisposition of the natural environment towards her. This is not just the mad raving of a character uprooted from her urban comfort zone back in Glasgow; her impending sacrifice is couched in Christ-like terms as she confides her fevered identification with Christ's martyrdom to Alec Webster the grocer, before in the end she atones for her husband's perfidy with her life. The notion of alien forces assuaged by redemptive sacrifice is asserted in the closing lines of the story where, following the discovery of Ellen's body, Alec Webster corroborates Ellen's conviction that she was in the grip of extraordinary natural forces as he apprehends 'the green hills that stood to peer with quiet faces in the blow of the wind from the sunset's place' (*Sm*34).

The comedy gold of the second published Gibbon story 'Smeddum' is palpably less ambitious though no less successful, administering typically witty censure for one of the author's pet hates: the vice of hypocrisy. Published in *The Scots Magazine* in January of 1933, this, the most anthologised Gibbon story, manufactures a glorious comic turnaround in which the hypocritical offspring of the irrepressible figure of Meg Menzies are duly punished at the tale's climax that discloses that their mother had enjoyed the independence from accepted *mores* that she indulges in youngest daughter Kathie and neglected to solemnise her own relationship with their father by formal means of marriage. Mitchell is in his element in 'Smeddum', squarely establishing Meg Menzies's farm of Tocherty Toun in his fictional heartland of Kinraddie, with Segget within view of the main farm and with the Mearns towns of Kinneff, Inverbervie and Stonehaven forming a convincing real-life topography for the action. Again the action is submersed in Mitchell's beautifully realised farming setting, while the discreet idiomatic Scots proves a superb medium for comedy: the titular quality of 'smeddum' perfectly captures the formidable strength of character of Meg Menzies, one of Gibbon's single most glorious creations whose fearsomeness as the family matriarch who physically bullies her errant siblings into structured propriety is tempered by her soft spot for her indolent husband Will and for Kathie her rebellious daughter, both of whom are granted exemption from her iron rule. Memorably dubbed 'rampageous and ill with her tongue' (*Sm*36), Meg's raucous dialogue crackles from the pages, for example in her combative riposte to the grocer's expressions of concern for her in her apparent dotage:

> *Damn the age! But I've finished the trauchle of the bairns at last, the most of them married or still over young. I'm as swack as ever I was, my lad. But I've just got the notion to be a bit sweir.* (*Sm*41, italics in original text)

The story's structure reveals Gibbon as a master of the form, as he plants evenly spaced steppingstones as clues to Meg's apparent inconsistency in her treatment of Will and of Kathie. This all culminates in the beautiful confluence in the denouement between her free-thinking decision to defer formal marriage to Will and her liberated endorsement of daughter Kathie's equally radical flouting of conformity in emigrating to Canada with John Robb without solemnising their relationship. The slap in the face delivered to Meg's querulous brood convened to reprove Kathie is suitably crisp, as in the sting at the tail they discover to their mortification that they all have been born out of wedlock.

'Clay', the final *Scots Magazine* piece from February 1933, is the most successful of all the Gibbon stories and one of Mitchell's most intimately meaningful works, constituting an excellent foil for 'Greenden' in giving a sanguine impression of nature's overweening influence on the human realm – although its effect isn't wholly benign. The story of Rob Galt's compulsive pursuit of his farming vocation has all the elementalism of Mitchell's best writing, drawing on his fascination for ancient history pursued in his adolescence in the fields and hills back at Arbuthnott and, in the portrayal of Galt's singular devotion to the land of Pittaulds, directly capitalising on the comprehensive knowledge of crofting farmers and their work derived from his upbringing. Characterisation and setting are grounded and earthy, as the story moves from dramatisation of the domestic intrigue of Rob Galt's family to the unfolding story of a wife and daughter abandoned in the anti-hero's unrelenting drive to maximise the arable potential of his farm. Mitchell's insider knowledge of agricultural practices is employed to dynamic effect in the narrator's charting of Rob Galt's compulsion, as he explores every conceivable practical means of both optimising the yield of his existing fields and of breaking in waste land – arduous tasks that his father had faced in real life in his battle for survival at both Auchterless and Arbuthnott. The author's warm personification of Rob's land reflects the protagonist's almost sensual rapport with his subject, while the attention that he pays to his fields by counterpoint shows up his growing neglect of his wife, increasingly needful of his attention in her terminal cancer, and of his daughter, aching after paternal interest and yet denied even basic financial support for college. Mitchell's evocation of Rob's farming labours has all the spontaneity of first-hand experience, inviting some sympathy with the main character, and Rob's only daughter Rachel is the perfect vehicle for articulation of a philosophical theme that was close to the author's heart, finally investing the lowly clay soil – the very substance that so bedevilled her father's endeavours – with deep symbolic meaning. Rachel's closing vision has the authority of the most incisive of Chris Guthrie's epiphanies, as she finds in the working and re-working of nature a sense of universal harmony, reflecting: 'All life – just clay that awoke and strove to return again to its mother's breast' (*Sm*80). At the very close finally she apprehends that her father's death has marked the end of an era, plangently fusing the human and the natural as she finds 'the earth turn sleeping, unquieted no longer, her hungry bairns in her hungry breast where sleep and death and the earth were one' (*Sm*81). The lyricism of Chris Guthrie's demise couldn't be more cogently approximated.

'Sim', a rogue story by Gibbon from *The Free Man* in June 1933, is the most neglected of the four rural stories, although it's every bit as tightly constructed as 'Smeddum', boasting an equally dominant central character in the inveterately aspirational Sim, darkly comic plot and an equally meaningful kick at the end hammering home the cautionary message satirising wanton capriciousness and unrestrained self-interest. Mitchell is afforded less scope in 'Sim' for the representation of Mearns society or of agricultural work, but his specialist knowledge of the local farming structures and roles and of the kind of holdings that his protagonist inhabits lends credibility to the narrative. Sim Wilson is the fictional personification of 'sweir' in that, far from Rob Galt's monomania, his labours are triggered by ulterior motivation, the shortcomings of his outlook being writ large in the ephemerality of successive short-term targets. Sim is presented as a figure of ridicule, as his default setting of open indolence is interrupted by periodic bouts of calculated guile and hyperactivity: his will to succeed at school is sparked off by the ambition to win a cash prize; his industry at the farm of Upperhill is predicated on his aim to win the hand of the girl of his dreams by taking over his own farm at Haughgreen; his reversion to type at the farm is corrected by his wish to do his best by his prized daughter Jean; his relapse following discovery of his first daughter's learning disability is arrested by the doting paternal desires swiftly transferred to his second daughter Jess. With jubilant poetic justice, at the story's climax Jean unwittingly draws attention to her little sister's pregnancy, subsequently detonating her parents' shame, with Sim's closing humiliation representing just punishment for his moral turpitude. 'Sim' is thus a marvellously Scottish study in miniature of the hubristic rise and fall of the self-made man who is the tale's protagonist, a scenario that's archly indebted to the example of *The House with the Green Shutters* and *Hatter's Castle*.

As is the case with the component novels of the trilogy, the more poetically appealing setting of the rural stories populated with a more manageable cast of rounded characters has unfairly overshadowed the shorter fiction using the more unforgiving locus of the modern city. 'Forsaken' was a radical new departure for Grassic Gibbon at this time, as a bulletin dispatched straight from the heart of the modern Scottish city grimly dramatising Christ's second coming when he pitches up in the very midst of an everyday proletarian family that signally fails to recognise his Christ-like qualities, of love, of faith, which have become inimical to the moral climate of the times. The unfamiliar harshness of the dialect shows Mitchell experimenting with the narrative mode that he employed to more sustained effect towards the end of the year in *Grey Granite,* and 'Forsaken' in fact endorses the severe politics promulgated later through Ewan's characterisation at the end of the third volume of the trilogy, as a desperate measure required for desperate times. Having stuck with his winning formula for the first four Gibbon stories, therefore, the author rings wholesale changes for his last one, as a much higher tariff production. First published in *Scottish Scene* just five months before *Grey Granite,* 'Forsaken' is in fact Gibbon's most ambitious story, experimenting for the first time with an unpalatably harsh urban setting and melding this heavily realised modern world with the miraculous fantasy of Christ's second coming represented in resolutely non-miraculous terms.

Mitchell regularly toyed with the humanised image of Christ presented as a figure of radical political import, from the graphic representation of the crucifixion featured in his first novel to the whimsical conversation staged between Chris and Robert in *Cloud Howe* in which Chris speculates on the ambivalent response that the second coming would elicit among the Scottish people, coupling spontaneous kindness and prickly rumour-mongering regarding the cause of his stigmata. The seeds were sown for the final Gibbon short story.

The narrative mode in 'Forsaken' anticipates the heteroglossic narrative of *Grey Granite,* although it's more controlled, interweaving seven distinct sensibilities, from Christ himself, semi-jocularly humanised by his lapsing into idiomatic Scots, to the five members of the Gordon family and Johnny Tamson, young Pete's mischievous pal. Instantly, the exposition drops the reader into Christ's confusion, disorientated by the sufferings of his past and disconcerted by the mysterious present that he has now been cast adrift in. His take on humankind appears objectively fair, if unexpectedly unromanticised, as he owns to 'seeing the filth and the foolishness in folk, but the kindly glimmer of the spirit as well' (*Sm*46).

Christ is introduced to the contemporary reality of the Scottish city first of all through his encounter with Pete and Johnny, accepting the stranger as an exotic immigrant and keen to protect him from victimisation as a 'Yid' – a brief insight to the unsettled race relations developing between the wars and to the escalating anti-semitism insidiously creeping throughout Europe (the odious anti-semitic programme of the German Nazi Party can be formally traced to 1933, with the passing of repressive legislation against the Jews). Invited home with father Peter, the stranger thereafter is treated with due kindness by the Gordons who, very like the Watsons in *Grey Granite*, emerge as a typical working-class family with individual interests and concerns, including Will's hard-line radicalism as secretary of the local Communist cadre and his father's quaintly old-fashioned philanthropic approach to social and political issues.

Mitchell also draws an elaborate allegorical connection between the individual Gordon family members and Christ's former followers, with Peter representing the biblical disciple, Ma standing for Martha, Jess representing Mary Magdalene and Will representing Saul. The parallel continuity in characterisation is perhaps just too pat, and yet it serves to highlight the profound changes that have taken place in society in the interim, which in turn have engendered fundamental changes in people's outlook – and Will's unavailing efforts to apprise the stranger of the legend of Jesus Christ shows ironically how far the Christian message has strayed in the intervening period since his lifetime. Christ's disillusionment mirrors the perilous state of the world that he has returned to, where the pure love that he had inspired has now assumed an emphatically dissonant character. His conclusion is inescapable as he apprehends a normal, spontaneously welcoming family stripped of their more elevated feelings by the desperate circumstances that they have now inherited in the modern city. Grown impatient with gradualism, Will is Ewan Tavendale in waiting, his soul now bereft of former noble feelings, of love, faith, trust, hope, all forgone in his single-minded political resolve. Paradoxically, Ma's modern incarnation appears most forlorn of all, as Christ senses her spiritual emptiness, 'facing fear and pain without hope' (*Sm*57).

Christ's departure eloquently symbolises his alienation in the face of the sinister urban reality of the 1930s. His final cry of despair, transliterated from Aramaic, *'Eloi! Eloi! lama sabachthani?'* (*Sm*46, italics in original text) – 'My God! My God! Why hast thou forsaken me?' – the biblical epigraph inscribed at the start of the story capturing Christ's anguished abandonment by man and God at his crucifixion, now acquires a topical urgency as his former hosts fail even to recognise the words, let alone to decode their traditional significance.

'Forsaken' has the same astringent political temper as *Grey Granite*, advocating revolutionary political activism as the only viable response to the desperation of the inter-war years. In many ways the story also constitutes a trial run for the technical sophistry of the urban novel, representing the single most ambitious work of fiction published under the Gibbon pen name. Christ is vividly identified as a human being through his resurrection in the midst of a modern Scottish family of appreciable ordinariness, through the juxtaposing of his slowly untangling historical memories with the Gordon family's everyday concerns and through his own accessibly demotic vernacular. The genre-defying experiment with abruptly shifting narrative voices, with harsh urban dialect, with extended allegory, with a symmetrical framework relaying untranslated biblical borrowings, makes extreme demands on the reader – demands that in the end are handsomely rewarded.

Mitchell was a witty essayist, who deserved to win the kind of generous financial retainer that was commanded by respected columnists earning favour in the London literary scene from the 1920s onwards, such as JB Priestley, Compton Mackenzie and Arnold Bennet, who churned out 'middle articles', amusing thousand-word meditations on almost any subject expressly tailored for the new calibre of casual readers thirsty for undemanding diversion. The Grassic Gibbon essays in *Scottish Scene* are models of their kind, stylishly written pieces that are by turn witty and passionate and thought-provoking, granting fresh insight on a diverse range of Scottish subjects and all yielding fascinating access to the author's background and thinking.

As has already been seen, the autobiographical essays on 'The Land', 'Aberdeen' and 'Glasgow' provide a chronological index to the author's earlier life; the remainder, on 'The Antique Scene', 'The Wrecker – James Ramsay MacDonald', 'Literary Lights' and 'Religion', tell the reader just about as much about the writer's deepest held opinions and beliefs in a stylishly rumbustious fashion. Adopting a calculatedly opinionated stance (although this was the normal default position of Mitchell's Scots persona anyway), the author habitually splits Scotland's past and present into the two main socio-political factions, of rulers and oppressed – the division that dominated his whole world picture. MacDiarmid's essays in fact appear even more vitriolic than the Gibbon ones; his devil-may-care tone is most evident in the study of 'Politicians', lacing the base-line name-checking with quite savage insults – and this is after the Jarrolds legal department had done its work.

Mitchell's mature writing is a riot of left-wing ideology constantly governed by the overriding concern with justice and fairness. The writer is best understood when his thinking is viewed through the twin axis of the two key autobiographical essays in *Scottish Scene*, on 'The Land' and 'Glasgow', written with verve and vehemence about the contrasting environs of country and city. The first essay represents the unfettered passions of the born peasant, demonstrating the author's unrivalled capacity to capture and interrogate the bittersweetness of the peasant's love–hate relationship with the land, veering from an inclination to sentimentality towards a more reserved sympathy for the rural workers. Mitchell's motivational humanism is fully captured in the climax of the essay, where he exclaims:

> I am unreasonably and mulishly prejudiced in favour of my own biological species. I am a jingo patriot of planet earth: 'Humanity right or wrong!' (*Sm*95)

Neatly divided into four sections titled according to the four seasons echoing the structuring of *Sunset Song*, 'The Land' is absolutely central to an understanding of Mitchell's response to his rural heritage. His memories move from fond childhood experiences, snugly happed in his mother's shawl on the harvest field, to his recent nostalgic holiday back at Arbuthnott in September of 1933, which feeds in directly to the section titled 'Summer'. Here, he recalls a day trip that was tantamount to a personal pilgrimage, taking stock of the increase in the local grasslands, of the parks and the bogs replacing the lost woods and lamenting the effects that the modern environmental changes have wrought on the local wildlife. He retraces the lulling mindfulness of his bicycle ride through the Glen of Drumtochty and up to the top of Cairn o' Mount, the loftiest viewpoint scanning the whole splendid panorama of the Mearns right over to Angus, where he finds the spiritual tranquillity for ruminating on rural life, on agriculture and nature – inspiring one of the most affecting passages in the book (*Sm*89–93). The essay is in fact startlingly modern in its green politics, with Mitchell's conception of the Land, as signifying an ecologically balanced and harmonious combination of people and place, sustaining a fairly radical political agenda that focuses on the social plight of the peasantry committed to working their smallholdings. There is absolutely no romantic neo-pastoralism in evidence here.

Mitchell's publisher Robert Hale had recommended that the authors between them should carve up the four major Scottish cities and write profiles of them as a ruse to attract sales, and he got much more than he bargained for, particularly in the Gibbon essays on Aberdeen and Glasgow, which combine autobiographical reflection with knowledgeable reportage, always augmented with astute discourse on intensely serious social, political and cultural issues. 'Glasgow' captures the author's trenchant engagement with topical social and political concerns, concerns that had become much more acute as the 1920s moved into the 1930s. In this highly polemical essay Mitchell dedicates his whole aesthetic to the political cause of ridding Scottish society of its deepest ills – a mission whose moral compulsion goes way beyond national identities, and that indeed ultimately forces recognition of the potentially constraining effects of conceptions of nationhood. In his most mature essay on the role of the revolutionary writer in *Left Review* at the end of his life Mitchell spelt out the revolutionary writers' collective function as being to constitute 'a shock brigade of writers'. His own strategic tendency to 'shout too loudly' bursts to the fore here, achieving an all-embracing conviction in his indictment of the poverty and degradation rife in deprived conurbations in Glasgow that had become infamous throughout

Europe for appalling insanitary conditions and overcrowding, which moves him to declare almost evangelically:

> There is nothing in culture or art that is worth the life and elementary happiness of one of those thousands who rot in the Glasgow slums. (*Sm*102)

Leslie Mitchell's mature ideology transcended time and place, and his native land was subject to exaction of the self-same humanist principles that dominated his thinking and his writing as a whole. While Scottish artists and writers rallied to the nationalist cause with increasing zeal throughout the 1930s, though, Mitchell was chary about conflating the political and cultural claims of the movement. Never one to be hidebound by political decorum, nationalism is comprehensively vilified in 'Glasgow', where he exclaims with deliberate hyperbole, 'What a curse to the earth are small nations!' (*Sm*106) and rejects nationalism and internationalism, perceived as 'twin halves of an idiot whole', in favour of 'ultimate cosmopolitanism' (*Sm*108), an essentially anarchist ideal of an apolitical state safeguarding global unity, individual freedom and universal equality. Mitchell's radical political convictions had crystallised with admirable clarity.

The essay on 'Aberdeen' is a beautifully nuanced homage to his local city that he lived in on two separate occasions, as a boy and a young adult, pinning down the enigmatic qualities that the Silver City by the Sea held for him, as 'the one haunting and exasperatingly lovable city in Scotland' (*Sm*122). However, his deftly humorous recount of his experiences there focuses exclusively on his time as a garrulous young reporter and wallows in his callow adventures throughout the last year of the war, assigned as a journalist to an insalubrious beat down at the docks, fascinated and horrified by the war's effects on the home front and inspired by the international fallout from the Russian Revolution – which fleetingly touched his reporter's rounds at Aberdeen harbour as he encountered Bolshevik apparatchiks stopping off on their repatriation back to their motherland – to join the newly formed Aberdeen Soviet. The 1934 portrait teases out the ambivalences of the city location, as ever sharply divided into the respectable and deprived neighbourhoods, and of the inhabitants curiously fusing urban cosmopolitanism and rustic couthieness. His portrait is filled with affection informed by an understanding of the physical factors that have moulded the Aberdonians' dourly indomitable character: the inhospitable climate inherited from proximity to the North Sea and the widespread use in housing of the local grey granite, apprehended as 'starkly grim and uncompromising' (*Sm*111) – exactly like young Ewan's characterisation in the novel. The humorous passage describing the outlandish calorific overkill of the local high tea provides welcome relief from the serious social commentary concentrating on the poor and the downtrodden and on the piecemeal nature of the political representation of their cause.

Ramsay MacDonald, historically a figure of hate for the radical left, earns a dismissive reference in 'Aberdeen', and Mitchell expanded on this in 'The Wrecker – James Ramsay MacDonald', a vigorous character assassination tracing the failure of the contemporary Labour movement to the political shortcomings embodied by MacDonald's career in deserting the fight for social justice and shifting the parliamentary party to the right of centre, ostensibly in the effort to wrest power from the Conservatives – a cosy centralism replicated half a century later by Tony Blair. Mitchell's essay has a biting perspicacity as he balances acknowledgement of MacDonald's early principled opposition to the First World War and his prowess as a parliamentarian with acrimonious denunciation of the first Labour prime minister on account of his political moderatism. The condemnation of MacDonald's first reactionary Labour Government of 1923 gives way to censure of the notoriously anaemic opposition posed in the General Strike, which Mitchell casts as the prelude to MacDonald's dereliction of his political duties as head of the National Government – and the prelude effectively to the Labour party's demise as primary representative of the subaltern classes. Mitchell's trenchant review of the strike and of the sacrilegious failure of the Labour party to lend it their support carries on where *Cloud Howe* left off.

The Gibbon essays on 'Religion' and 'The Antique Scene' are more tendentious in their orientation. The essay on religion begins by trotting out the fundamental Diffusionist axiom that institutionalised religion is an unnatural and unwanted phenomenon and argues in typically forthright terms that in a Scottish context the power of the church is anachronistic and misguided, misleading the ordinary people in wartime and in peacetime. While he savours 'the lovely poetry of the Bible', in 'a book that can be as painfully wearying as it can be painfully enthralling' (*Sm*161–2), Mitchell doesn't spare the kirk for its pernicious influence on Scottish morality – an unpopular argument that won Grassic Gibbon notoriety with the Scottish establishment, as well as invaluable publicity. The opposition of the rote observance pursued in the services in the Church of Scotland to the spontaneous joyfulness of the natural world has a deeply personal motivation, while the prediction of the demise of formal church worship among the waves of socio-political developments to come throws up a topically fearful aside capturing the author's enduring suspicion of nationalism:

> What has happened in Italy and Germany may happen in Scotland. The various Scots nationalist parties have large elements of Fascism within them. There is now a definite Fascist Party. (*Sm*165–6)

The essay on 'The Antique Scene', a highly individualised overview of the development of the Scottish nation, also falls prey to the author's unfettered Diffusionist tendencies, although the generic pattern that Scotland is shoehorned into, of 'Colonisation, Civilisation, and Barbarisation' (*Sm*3), has much in common with the post-colonial meme put forward by modern cultural historians such as Frantz Fanon and Edward Said. An acute sense of class consciousness pervades Mitchell's historical perspective, as famous people and events from ancient to modern times are judged in accordance with their ultimate effect on the 'common' folk. There are few bright spots in his brisk litany of national disasters, from the racial conflicts between Picts and Kelts (Celts) and with invading Angles, Romans and Norsemen, up through the Battle of Flodden, the Reformation and the Covenanters' resistance to the Union of the Crowns, the calamitous Darien Scheme and Union of the Parliaments, up to the Jacobite rebellions and the ultimate emblem of the tragic confusion of Scottish history, the defeat of Prince Charles Edward Stuart at the Battle of Culloden. Certain events are savoured for their egalitarian and libertarian spirit, principally the War of Independence led by Mitchell's iconic freedom fighter

William Wallace, which is applauded as a corrective to 'the nationalism forced upon an unwilling or indifferent people by the intrigues of kings or courtesans' and that involves instead 'the spontaneous uprising of an awareness of blood-brotherhood and freedom-right' (*Sm*12). The closing peroration brings the picture right up to date in a spirited Marxist critique of the destructive capitalist economics of the modern era:

> It is a hundred and fifty years of unloveliness and pridelessness, of growing wealth and growing impoverishment, of Scotland sharing in the rise and final torturing maladjustments of that economic system which holds all the modern world in thrall. (*Sm*22)

'Literary Lights', Mitchell's survey of Scotland's literature, illustrates just how quickly the author had come up to speed with the native tradition, and, barring odd lapses, broadly speaking he is secure in his judgement of individual writers, brazenly singling out the joint authors of *Scottish Scene* as the most important and ambitious practitioners in the field of modern Scottish literature. The passages focusing on the key concerns of the Scottish writer, particularly with regard to the fundamental choice of utilising Scots or Scots language variants as opposed to more orthodox English-based alternatives, astutely highlight the main predicaments vexing Scottish novelists and poets as a whole – the central issue of language choice later becoming a politico-cultural battleground that gave rise to ferocious debate and that shortly afterwards was to cause a deeply personal rift between the aggressively anglophobic Hugh MacDiarmid and confirmed anglophile Edwin Muir. As mentioned previously, Mitchell sets out his own ambition for Scottish writing in suitably aspirational terms, as he talks of the ultimate aim of hailing the emergence of 'a Scots Joyce, a Scots Proust' (*Sm* 124). This accurately reflects the exalted scale of his modernist remit in the Grassic Gibbon fiction in particular, in recognising the potentiality that a literary form of Scots possessed to create fiction of the very highest order to match MacDiarmid's remarkable achievement as the grandee of modern Scots poetry.

8

Legacy

Leslie Mitchell moved progressively further away from his roots from early adulthood and travelled widely throughout the world in search of personal fulfilment without ever fully appreciating what lay closest to his heart – the people and countryside simply embodied in the conceptualisation of 'the Land' that emotionally he struggled to come to terms with throughout his short life. Piecing his life story together, he seems now an extraordinary figure who had to endure uniquely turbulent times and who had a persistently uneasy relationship with his immediate social circumstances, as a classic 'lad o' pairts' denied the kailyard-style happy ending to his hard-won success with a shockingly sudden death. Curiously, the tragedy of Mitchell's early death has only served to consolidate his semi-legendary status in the eyes of the public, along with doomed geniuses such as Keats, Shelley and Burns prefiguring the lionisation of rock celebrities in modern times who have died in mid-career, leaving the perennial 'what if' question hanging tantalisingly unanswered.

Following his death, Ray Mitchell worked assiduously to preserve her husband's personal legacy as a happy family man, dedicating herself to the arduous task of bringing up their children throughout the war years while returning to her post at the Post Office Savings Bank in London, having resisted the initial temptation to return to Scotland. Mitchell's wealth at death amounted to just over £300 (around £16,000 today), and apart from *A Scots Quair* and *Spartacus* that earned swift re-publication as cheap Jackdaw paperbacks, his books quickly fell out of print. However, invaluable short-term financial assistance came through in due course in the form of a collection from fellow writers organised by the Scottish PEN Club in Edinburgh, a grant from The Royal Literary Fund and, later, a Civil List Pension.

Despite the snowballing list of works that he had been stacking up and the generous file of synopses left extant among his papers, Leslie Mitchell left no completed typescripts unpublished at his death. His widow's efforts to drum up interest with Alexander Korda and other film directors to produce money-spinning films of *Sunset Song* and *The Lost Trumpet* unfortunately proved unsuccessful, and the subsequent failure to place *Spartacus* was particularly galling in light of the runaway success achieved by Stanley Kubrick's 1960 Hollywood epic starring Kirk Douglas, based instead on Howard Fast's novel, which would have brought all her financial troubles to an end.

After decades of futile wrangling with publishers Ray Mitchell began to observe a revival in her husband's reputation in the late 1960s. *A Scots Quair*, as had been anticipated, has never fallen out of print, and its reputation has steadily grown over the years, at home and abroad. A belated revival of interest in Mitchell's other works was sparked off by Ian S Munro's biography from 1966, which helped to further his reputation and produced two useful spin-offs, with the release in 1967 of *A Scots Hairst*, Munro's compendium of shorter Mitchell and Gibbon pieces culled from *Scottish Scene* and elsewhere, followed up by welcome republication of *Spartacus* by Hutchinson in 1970. A schools edition of *Sunset Song* released in 1971 on the back of the groundswell of interest in Scottish devolution also spawned popular paperback reprints of the three novels of the trilogy from Pan Books in 1973. Since Ray Mitchell's death in 1978, Rhea Martin seamlessly carried on her mother's legacy as the keeper of the flame, working assiduously behind the scenes to foster interest in her father's writing by students, academics and publishers and in the media. In addition, together with her brother Daryll Mitchell she remained faithful to her Scottish heritage, maintaining contact with relations in the Mearns and the north of Scotland; the generosity of Mitchell's son and daughter helped to bring the local memorialisation of the Grassic Gibbon Centre into being in 1992, marking the final rehabilitation of their father's reputation in his homeland.

The capacity of Gibbon's masterpiece to make the crossover

to different genres has long been recognised in practice, with varying degrees of success. Radio adaptations of *Sunset Song* and *Cloud Howe* broadcast on the Scottish Home Service in 1948 and 1953 respectively paved the way for later dramatisations of the stories 'Smeddum', 'Sim', 'Clay' and 'Greenden' on the BBC Home Service from October 1966 to February 1967. Most prominently, the televised version of the trilogy produced by BBC Scotland found a whole new audience for the novels; Vivien Heilbron's fondly remembered performance as Chris Guthrie, running from 1971's *Sunset Song* through *Cloud Howe* in 1982 and *Grey Granite*, finally broadcast in 1983, provided for many viewers the authoritative physical likeness of Gibbon's heroine. The stories *Clay, Smeddum and Greenden*, adapted as a BBC1 'Play for Today' in 1976, featuring Eileen McCallum's unforgettable performance as the redoubtable Meg Menzies in *Smeddum*, advanced her reputation exactly as the trilogy had done previously for Heilbron's. In recent times the reappearance of *A Scots Quair* on BBC radio reaffirmed the narrative immediacy of Gibbon's heavily verbalised style, with *Sunset Song* appearing on its own in 1996 and later being aired in a different production in 2009 before *Cloud Howe* followed in 2015. The most lavish adaptation of Gibbon's works to date is auteur Terence Davies's long-awaited film of *Sunset Song*, finally released in 2015. Unfortunately, while Davies's highly vaunted film version introduced Gibbon's writing to new audiences, his expurgation of some of the author's central themes in his script – particularly the book's urgent socio-political message – compromises the impact of the end product.

Gibbon's fiction also has a long-standing affinity with the stage, testifying again to the narrative verve of his prose style. Ian S Munro directed a condensed version of *Sunset Song* in Aberdeen in May 1964, but it was TAG Theatre's muscular rendition of Alastair Cording's adaptation of all three components of the trilogy in the 1990s – regularly revived in later years – that made the strongest case for Grassic Gibbon's ability to make this dramatic transition while remaining faithful to the original texts.[1]

Book-length studies of Mitchell have been surprisingly few and far between, although following Ian S Munro's original biography from 1966, they have proved arrestingly diverse in their critical representation of the author's inner life. Douglas

F Young's *Beyond the Sunset* (1973) offered a pioneering critical overview measured against the author's consuming interest in Diffusionism. The 1980s signified a mini-revival of interest, in the form of three diverse studies, with Douglas Gifford in 1983 producing an invigorating comparison with Neil Gunn within the cultural context of the Modern Scottish Literary Renaissance, the present author's monograph from 1984 setting the primary and secondary works within a broad ideological framework and Ian Campbell the following year covering his life and works with astute economy. In the following decade Uwe Zagratzki produced in 1991 a thoroughgoing analysis of Mitchell's utopian politics (unfortunately only available as a German-language text) and Peter Whitfield uncovered some fresh biographical and historical details in his brief monograph from 1994, while Clarke Geddes's fictionalised account of Mitchell's life in 1996 is memorable for identifying the significance of Inverbervie as a key biographical influence behind the setting of *Cloud Howe*. In the present century a lull followed the appearance in 2003 of Christoph Ehland's focused structuralist examination of the picaresque in *The Thirteenth Disciple* and *Image and Superscription* before the present writer's *Lewis Grassic Gibbon: A Revolutionary Writer* from 2016 offered a brief conspectus of Mitchell's writing as a whole set against the social, cultural and political backdrop of his life and times.

In his lifetime Mitchell's books divided the critics across the political spectrum and the conversation was invariably governed by political rather than aesthetic factors. Critics of nationalist and left-wing inclination have fought fiercely for his soul, with battle being joined principally over *A Scots Quair*. In recent years the republication of *Stained Radiance*, *The Thirteenth Disciple*, *Spartacus* and *Gay Hunter* has led to their critical rediscovery, adding markedly to Mitchell's literary stature. However, *A Scots Quair* has steadily grown with the years, finding ever greater acclaim with a mass audience and with academics at home and abroad; in recent times the adoption of *Sunset Song* as a set text by the Open University in 2005 and its publication as a Penguin Classic in 2007 have consolidated the reputation of Grassic Gibbon beyond Scotland – although this has perpetuated the injustice thrown up by a serial approach to the trilogy, whereby *Sunset Song*'s popularity overshadows the remaining volumes and obscures the work's formal integrity as a single unit.

Lewis Grassic Gibbon and *A Scots Quair* quickly became fixtures in generalist histories of Scottish literature, beginning with William Power's *Literature and Oatmeal*, commissioned by Gibbon himself as general editor for Routledge's Voice of Scotland series and published just after his death, which in under 200 pages provides a wide-ranging comparative survey of the Scottish literary tradition (including Gaelic literature), reserving a suitably auspicious, justly politicised, space for Grassic Gibbon, as 'a passionate idealist who, had he lived, would have played a leading part in the social revival of Scotland'.[2] Two decades later the German critic Kurt Wittig produced a much needed objective overview of the distinctive characteristics of the Scottish literary tradition, and while he preferred Gunn to Gibbon as the finest practitioner in the field of modern Scottish fiction, he balanced his traditionalist view of the trilogy's creative deterioration in *Grey Granite* with a fresh unpacking of the multi-layered richness of its overall achievement, dealing simultaneously with the personal, social and mythical levels, finally forming 'the most ambitious single effort in Scottish fiction'.[3] A further twenty years on Maurice Lindsay followed this triadic predilection to interpret the trilogy in terms of layers of meaning; worse, his introductory gambit centring on the throwaway remark that 'there is nothing humorous about *A Scots Quair*' appears woefully remiss, given the elements of irony, satire, black humour, farce and even slapstick that distinguish Gibbon's fiction voice.[4] American Francis Russell Hart, Gunn's official biographer together with JB Pick, set the record straight to some extent when he reserved a prominent place for Leslie Mitchell in his chapter on 'Novelists of the Modern Renaissance' in his comprehensive study of *The Scottish Novel* in 1978, broadening the perspective to take in Mitchell's other novels evoking narrative echoes of the trilogy (with an especially astute appraisal of *Spartacus*), as well as flagging up his innovations with style and his ideological influence by Diffusionism. Hart repudiates the previous tendency of critics such as Wittig and Lindsay to deconstruct the trilogy compartmentally, and while he convinces with his rejection of this mode of approach and with his contention that the volume's frame of reference extends way beyond the Scottish tradition, his negligence of the left-wing political urgency of the book is regrettable.[5]

From the 1980s onwards Scottish literary criticism has engendered increasingly generous – and sensitive – appraisals of Gibbon's legacy. Two volumes dealing with the Scottish literary tradition appearing in quick succession in 1983 offered a broader take on Mitchell's achievement. In *The Macmillan Companion to Scottish Literature* Trevor Royle gave due credit to the influence of Diffusionism on his philosophy and his writing.[6] Alan Bold, meanwhile, unfortunately relaying as gospel Mitchell's fabrication that he studied Mayan antiquities in situ in Central America, devoted sixteen pages in his study *Modern Scottish Literature* to analysing even more fully *The Thirteenth Disciple* and *Spartacus*, as well as the intellectual impact of Diffusionism in his fiction and non-fiction. The very full commentary on *A Scots Quair* again succumbs to the schematic tendency to disclose three layers of meaning across the volume, although Bold securely places *Sunset Song* within the Scottish kailyard and anti-kailyard tradition while giving due credit to the thematic coherence of the volume as a whole.[7] Just a year later, while he perpetuates the canard that one of Mitchell's RASC postings was to India, Roderick Watson skilfully sets the world of *Sunset Song* within the time-honoured British rural tradition encompassing the novels of Hardy and Lawrence while vouchsafing the view of the trilogy's structural cohesion and rehabilitating *Grey Granite* within Gibbon's oeuvre. Watson's attention to the subtle theme played out across the trilogy, of 'the spiritual antithesis between "masculine" authority and "feminine" sensitivity', is the most welcome critical advance made in his evaluation of Mitchell's work.[8] Towards the end of the decade Cairns Craig's final volume in the massive four-part critical anthology of *The History of Scottish Literature* appears to have slighted Mitchell by refusing him a discrete chapter to himself, where his compeers Gunn, Muir and MacDiarmid have individual chapters devoted to them (MacDiarmid even has two dedicated essays, on his earlier and later output). Setting critical partisanship aside, however, Mitchell actually finds sympathetic treatment across the volume, principally in Isobel Murray's revealing triple tracking of his 'self-consciously Scottish' career alongside those of his contemporaries Eric Linklater and Naomi Mitchison in the chapter on 'Novelists of the Renaissance' and in Manfred Malzahn's perceptive rehabilitation of *Grey Granite* within the comparatively neglected cultural framework of 'The Industrial Novel' in Scotland.[9]

The end of the century witnessed publication of Cairns Craig's invigorating study of *The Modern Scottish Novel*, which explores the development of the national tradition in the novel while examining the paradox of its positive contribution as a product of a peripheral culture to what is perceived to be the English monoculture. Gibbon's achievement is a constant touchstone in Craig's impressively wide-ranging study of his subject, and he valuably pins down the originality of Grassic Gibbon's protean fiction voice and the political ramifications of its evolution throughout the trilogy, establishing the centrality of the changing folk narrative as a marker of the survival of the community (albeit in a radically different form) caught in the throes of profound societal change. The perception of the 'historyless' world opposed to the 'false promise of history' identifies one of the key thematic dialectics of the volume.[10]

The present century has produced Robert Crawford's populist Penguin History of Scottish Literature, *Scotland's Books*, an admirably comprehensive overview of Scotland's literary traditions packed into 800 pages, which gives due attention to Gibbon's accomplishment in producing in the trilogy a volume that matches its socio-political fervour with stylistic originality (as with Craig, specifically linked with James Kelman's fiction in recent times), and most of all with its nuanced deployment of central female focalisation.[11] Most recently, Gerard Carruthers brings a refreshingly incisive modern critical perspective to bear on Gibbon's work in his *Critical Guide to Scottish Literature*, laying fresh emphasis upon the boldness of the author's damning treatment of the war and hailing his achievement with narrative beyond the Scottish tradition altogether, as 'one of the triumphs of British modernism'.[12] The rather perfunctory treatment of Gibbon in *The Cambridge Companion to Scottish Literature* edited by Carruthers with Liam McIlvanney in 2012 is attributable as much to the structural difficulties presented in accommodating him within the single relevant chapter, devoted to 'Hugh MacDiarmid and the Scottish Renaissance', as to any diminution of his inherent importance and influence within the Scottish literary tradition.[13]

Comparison of the two volumes of critical essays published on Lewis Grassic Gibbon in consecutive decades this century is highly instructive. Of the fourteen contributors to *A Flame in the Mearns* from 2003, all but one were based in Scotland. The essays deal with familiar territory in Gibbon studies – his narrative technique, his humanism, his radical politics – but indicate potentially fruitful lines of development elicited by his primary works: the modernist narrative method of the trilogy, the pivotal importance of *Grey Granite* in the history of the modern Scottish urban novel, and pre-eminently the revelatory feminist reading sustained by the trilogy. By 2015 only three of the nine contributors to *The International Companion to Lewis Grassic Gibbon* are of Scottish provenance; of the rest, two, refreshingly, have an academic locus in England while the remainder are based in Italy, USA, Denmark and Poland. The robust confidence of the analysis undertaken in the volume reflects the added value to which Mitchell, in his guise as Grassic Gibbon, is now entitled, having won international recognition on several critical fronts – as a trailblazing modernist, cultural nationalist, left-wing libertarian, champion of female rights and neo-Romantic visionary.

The bedrock of the trilogy's reputation lies in its status as a landmark in working-class fiction, in Scotland, in Britain, and indeed in a European context. Grassic Gibbon's urban novel claims direct kinship with crusading British novels of working-class experience stretching from early responses such as Dickens's *Hard Times* and Tressell's *The Ragged Trousered Philanthropists* up to hard-line 1930s proletarian fiction like Walter Greenwood's *Love on the Dole*, Walter Brierley's *Means-Test Man*, Dot Allan's *Hunger Strike*, James Barke's *Major Operation* and Lewis Jones's *Cwmardy*, while the whole subaltern thrust of the trilogy links it with European classics such as Zola's *The Earth*, Gorky's *Mother* and Silone's *Fontamara*. James Barke's radical appraisal of his friend's achievement in *Left Review* exactly a year after his death married personal insight with political understanding, paving the way for stringent Marxist critiques of the trilogy throughout the succeeding decades.[14] The translation of *A Scots Quair* in East Germany and Hungary in the

Cold War era was fullest testament to the revolutionary Marxist ideology at play in the volume, principally in the characterisation of Ewan Tavendale in *Grey Granite*.[15] Indeed throughout the twentieth century the critical perception of the trilogy – and particularly of the final volume – perpetually became snarled up in the changing perceptions of communism, as critics in Western democracies, or at least with democratic sympathies, sought to protect Grassic Gibbon's good name by distancing his achievement from the hard-line Stalinism prevailing in the Soviet Union, where political governance had strayed well away from the idealistic principles that enshrined the nation's birth and infancy.

While George Orwell's famous caveat about the artistic shortcomings commonly afflicting left-wing writing has more than a germ of truth, by any objective critical standards Mitchell escapes his criticism. He wasn't remarkable in championing the cause of the lowest social classes, especially in the 1930s; however, in contrast with Eric Blair, he both lived the life of ordinary people in country and city and developed the craftsmanship to make great literature from this experience. As a writer with a genuine common touch, the breadth of appeal that his writing claims is virtually unique, satisfying the diverse demands of both popular and academic readerships. Unlike many of Mitchell's left-wing contemporaries, his best fiction has a timeless appeal. There is a documentary fidelity to the Gibbon portrait of 1930s Scotland, but the ethical drive of the narrative is undeniable. Furthermore, his dissection of the Scottish and British realpolitik has resonances that are universal and that are endlessly topical: the trilogy provides equally damning correlatives for the reactionary excesses of the Thatcherite government of the 1980s, for New Labour's smoothly groomed self-interest from the 1990s, in contemporary times for the uneasy alliance of principles found in coalition government, for anonymous Liberal Democrat centralism and the neo-fascist xenophobia and populism of the British National Party (BNP) and UK Independence Party (UKIP) bulldogs, as well as for the tricky jostling of nationalist ideology for recognition within the political mainstream. Most convincing of all is the radical call for systemic political and economic change, away from neoliberal capitalism favouring private enterprise and self-interest towards an egalitarian system predicated on humanitarian principles catering equally for people of all genders and ethnicities, irrespective of social and educational background, political persuasion and spiritual and religious belief.

A *Scots Quair* has received widespread critical attention that has served to highlight the richness of his literary achievement.[16] Critical writing on Mitchell now appears in academic publications from all over the world, with continental Europe challenging home-grown analysis done in recent times in terms of both quantity and quality. In addition, foreign translations of Mitchell's major works have steadily emerged – in Japan, France, Italy, Russia, Galicia, Germany and, most recently, in Spain – reinforcing his world standing as a writer of the highest order. Recognition has been slow in England, however, where generalist studies of the novel in English tend to overlook the ground-breaking contribution of Mitchell and Gibbon to the field. Ian S Munro noted in his biography back in 1966 that Grassic Gibbon's work, in common with Scottish writing in general, had failed to receive due recognition in England,[17] and the Scots author's critical appeal evidently still proves elusive within the British hegemony. Mitchell's failure to convince Compton Mackenzie in 1932 to head up a movement to found a Scottish Academy of Letters on the Irish model partly explains why in terms of supposedly peripheral cultures Scottish literature per se is the poor neighbour to the Irish tradition, doughtily led by the formidable standard bearers of Yeats and Joyce.[18] Political self-determination is a major discriminating factor also in the cultural cachet held by the respective nations within Britain and even further afield, and *A Scots Quair* isn't alone in occupying an invidious position within modern canonical perceptions of the novel. Rather than being viewed as part of a plurinational British sovereignty, Scotland appears culturally diminished in relation to its southern neighbour. Gibbon's literary achievement ultimately falls between two critical stools, traditionally pigeonholed as a product of a marginalised culture and yet deprived of the compensatory attention and the protective safeguards customarily accorded to works representing minority cultures, an emasculating syndrome traced by Grassic Gibbon in his essay on 'The Antique Scene' to the Union of the Crowns and the Union of the Parliaments, signifying for him the loss of the distinctive cultural focus accompanying 'the absorption of the northern people into the polity and name of the southern' (*Sm*21), most succinctly summed up in recent times by postmodernist Scottish writer and artist Alasdair Gray as 'the nation being treated as a province'.[19]

The English novel admittedly is an increasingly complex beast to define, having moved away from the traditional idea of narrative formally employing the language common to highly literate writers and readers (with dialect usage apologetically sequestered within inverted commas) to a pluralist understanding of works encompassing a diversity of styles, language forms and fiction modes. As Adrian Poole has pointed out, Sir Walter Scott was not faced with the political and cultural soul searching that Leslie Mitchell inherited as a Scottish novelist in the 1930s, concerning issues of national identity and literary expression.[20] Mitchell took conscious steps to obviate the notional circumscription of his fiction in its historical, geographical, social and cultural assumptions. Even *Sunset Song*, the most specifically localised novel of the trilogy, transcends the limitations of its setting, resonating universally with the immediacy of its nature poetry, with its vibrantly realised characterisation and tragicomic tone, with the paradigmatic charting of the irreversible transformation of rural communities by the advance of inexorable socio-political and economic forces taking over the whole world. Mitchell's concerns about constrictions being visited on his anglophone audience by the deployment of a distinctively Scottish authorial persona writing about distinctively Scottish subjects, albeit in a suitably modulated idiomatic style, have been borne out by the restricted critical demographic that his work has found in the decades since his writings first appeared. Arnold Kettle was pretty much a voice in the wilderness in making mention of Gibbon in Volume 2 of his two-volume *An Introduction to the English Novel* in 1953,[21] but Raymond Williams belatedly revoked Mitchell's perennial exclusion from prescriptive Leavisite surveys of the great tradition in British literature in *The Country and the City* in 1973, pointing up Gibbon's eminence within both rural and urban traditions in the field of the British novel, drawing an illuminating comparison of Gibbon with DH Lawrence, representing *A Scots Quair* as the foremost chronicle of the militant politics of the 1930s and concluding, 'Grassic Gibbon is especially important, since he speaks for many who never got to speak for themselves in recorded ways.'[22] Subsequent studies of left-wing writing have steadily found Mitchell a magisterial, if rarefied, place at the heart of the revolutionary tradition in Britain, and in Europe. H Gustav Klaus spearheaded the rehabilitation proper of Mitchell's reputation, proclaiming *A Scots Quair* in 1978 'the outstanding Socialist prose work of the inter-war period'.[23] Klaus's discerning endorsement has been meaningfully embellished in subsequent single-volume studies of British left-wing writing, in David Smith's *Socialist Propaganda in the Twentieth-Century British Novel* (1978), Valentine Cunningham's *British Writers of the Thirties* (1988), Andy Croft's *Red Letter Days: British Fiction in the 1930s* (1990), Ian Haywood's *Working-Class Fiction: From Chartism to Trainspotting* (1997) and most recently in James Smith's *The Cambridge Companion to British Literature of the 1930s* (2019).[24] Yet all of these accolades notwithstanding, the political novel generally has lost prestige in the modern world – and Gibbon's achievement in his great trilogy undoubtedly has suffered accordingly. Indeed the genre of the novel as a whole sadly has lost the cultural primacy that it possessed just after the First World War, when political writers habitually turned to the art of fiction in order to reach out to a popular audience.

While the Scottish label itself has to some extent inhibited Grassic Gibbon's renown, in addition to its traditional representation as a Scottish epic and a left-wing classic, *A Scots Quair* has lent itself to a range of critical interpretations shedding fresh light on both its techniques and ideas. Feminist criticism has drawn attention to the nucleal deployment of an empathically realised central character who as a female challenges the conventional *mores* of the time and sustains a profound vision of humankind's intimacy with the natural universe.[25] Post-colonialist criticism has brought out the revisionist tendency in the author's historical perspective, with the blanket condemnation of civilisation as a whole and of the imperialist hunger after colonisation incorporating a more pointed indictment of the institutionalised persecution of indigenous peoples by the entitled minority.[26] And the audacious stylistic accomplishments with narrative focalisation and stream of consciousness and the placing of a progressive aesthetic agenda preserving and promoting the distilled essence of national heritage and culture within a generous international frame of reference wins Grassic Gibbon a secure place within twentieth-century modernism.[27]

Leslie Mitchell is a writer of compelling humanity and compassion, but also of arresting profundity. In the final assessment, he should be prized most of all as a writer for our times in his impassioned espousal of green values, as a classic exponent of what is now simply named ecofiction, a genre in which the protagonist communes with nature and draws spiritual succour from this source. Written in the century before the term ecofiction was even coined, *A Scots Quair* enshrines the author's deepest held beliefs about humankind and about our place in the universe. The critical mode of analysis known as ecocriticism draws out beautifully the most enduring refrains in Mitchell's writing, and in *A Scots Quair* in particular, integrating the twin concerns of social protest and environmental activism,[28] significantly with the deployment of a proto-feminist sensibility, as Timothy Clark has defined the intersectional connections within this modern critical discipline:

> Ecocriticism has plural strands, but this progressive commitment is almost universally shared. For most ecocritics, human abuse of the natural world is best understood as the corollary of unjust or oppressive systems of government and economics, and forms of social organisation (hierarchy, plutocracy, patriarchy) that both abuse other human beings and which have no hesitation taking a similar stance towards anything else. Traditions of feminism have been especially important here, tracing environmentally destructive behaviours to patriarchal norms of entitlement and ownership, and to fantasies of mastery both over nature and each other, in denial of human bodily finitude.[29]

The natural world is very much at the heart of Mitchell's writing, in the seminal essay on 'The Land' and in his major fiction. He brings to the normal mix of narrative ingredients a pronounced sense of place, and of its sublime influence on the human realm – emotionally, morally, socially, politically, spiritually. The affinity between people and place runs productively throughout his whole oeuvre; Chris Guthrie's lifelong quest to find ontological justification for her instinctual bond with the countryside dominates *Sunset Song* and the trilogy as a whole, mirroring the author's own innermost belief in the primacy of nature and of humankind's harmonious belonging within the organic world. Viewed in this way, *A Scots Quair* is a supremely life-affirming book, a narrative of passionate profundity speaking urgently for the present, and whose relevance ultimately transcends time.

Notes

CHAPTER 1: LIFE AND BACKGROUND

1. In 'Dear Robert', an autobiographical exercise in letter writing appearing in the middle book of three Arbuthnott School Essay Books preserved by his teacher Alexander Gray, the thirteen-year-old author considers: 'I think I will be a journalist, or perhaps an Editor' (NLS MS26106).
2. Ian Carter has appropriated the phrase, originally coined by the minister of Rayne in Aberdeenshire, as an apt subtitle for his detailed study of *Farm Life in Northeast Scotland 1840–1914: The Poor Man's Country* (Edinburgh: John Donald Publishers Ltd, 1979).
3. Letter, Mitchell to Alexander Gray, dated 29 September 1929, NLS MS26109.
4. Marc Edelman, 'What is a Peasant? What are Peasantries? A Briefing Paper on Issues of Definition'. Prepared for the first session of the Intergovernmental Working Group on a United Nations Declaration on the Rights of Peasants and Other People Working in Rural Areas, Geneva, 15–19 July 2013, available at http://www.ohchr.org/Documents/HRBodies/HRCouncil/WGPleasants/Edelman.pdf, retrieved on 8 June 2017.
5. Letter from Thomas Fotheringham, factor of Robert Gordon's College Lands, to Messrs Davidson & Garden, Aberdeen, dated 13 February 1908, in Arbuthnott Estate Papers, Arbuthnott Estate Rentals, tacks, etc., Aberdeen University Library GB0231 MS2764/2/2/1/50.
6. The Indian critic Ranajit Guha made the valuable distinction between the 'élite' and the 'subaltern classes', which he draws with specific reference to the days of the Raj, in 'On Some Aspects of the Historiography of Colonial India', *Selected Subaltern Studies*, edited by Ranajit Guha and Gahatri Chakravorty Spivak (New York: Oxford University Press, 1988), pp.37–44, p.44.
7. Formal documentation concerning James Mitchell's tenancy of Hillhead of Seggat is held at the archive of Robert Gordon's College in Aberdeen.

8. Arbuthnott Estate Papers, Estate development, construction and sales 1796–1928, 'Report upon and valuation of the Estates of Arbuthnott in the County of Kincardine' by A Agnew Ralston, Lindsay Howe & Co, February 1919, Aberdeen University Library MS2764/2/3/7.
9. Ian Shepherd, *Aberdeen and North-East Scotland*, Second Edition (Edinburgh: HMSO, 1996), pp.10–11, 23.
10. Arbuthnott Estates, Copy Conditions of Letting of The Farm of Bloomfield From Whitsunday 1908, 1908, Davidson & Garden, clause 6, pp.2–3, Aberdeen University Library GB0231 MS2764/2/2/1/40.
11. See in particular William Kenefick, *Red Scotland! The Rise and Fall of the Radical Left, c.1872 to 1932* (Edinburgh: Edinburgh University Press, 2007), Chapter 7.
12. 'Bolshevist Soviet in Aberdeen', *The Aberdeen Daily Journal*, Friday 20 December 2018, p.2.

CHAPTER 2. NARRATIVE PRELUDES: *THE CALENDS OF CAIRO* AND *PERSIAN DAWNS, EGYPTIAN NIGHTS*

1. Rudyard Kipling, 'The Ballad of East and West', *Collected Poems of Rudyard Kipling* (Ware: Wordsworth Editions, 1994), pp.245–8.
2. Among the wealth of histories written about relations between the West and the Middle East in this period, I have been most indebted to Piers Brendon's *The Decline and Fall of the British Empire 1781–1997* (London: Vintage, 2008); Niall Fergusson's *Empire: How Britain Made the Modern World* (London: Penguin, 2004); Robert Fisk's *The Great War for Civilization: The Conquest of the Middle East*, Revised Edition (London and New York: Harper Perennial, 2006); and, specifically concerning the Egyptian narrative, James Whidden's *Monarchy and Modernity in Egypt: Politics, Islam and Neo-colonialism Between the Wars* (Library of Middle East History) (London and New York: I.B. Tauris, 2013).

CHAPTER 3. THE REAL STUFF OF HISTORY: *HANNO, NIGER, THE CONQUEST OF THE MAYA* AND *NINE AGAINST THE UNKNOWN*

1. T.S. Eliot, 'Review of *The Growth of Civilisation* and *The Origin of Magic and Religion* by W. J. Perry', *The Criterion*, 2 (1924), pp.489–91, cited in Morag Shiach, 'Lewis Grassic Gibbon and Modernism', *The International Companion to Lewis Grassic Gibbon*, edited by Scott Lyall (Glasgow: Scottish Literature International, 2015), p.12.

2. Herbert Butterfield, *The Whig Interpretation of History* (London: G. Bell and Sons, 1931).
3. Lewis Grassic Gibbon, '"I Kent his Faither!" A Scots Writer Reviews his Reviewers', *Glasgow Evening News* (Saturday Supplement), 24 February 1934, p.1.
4. A useful guide to modern anthropological thinking is *The Routledge Encyclopaedia of Social and Cultural Anthropology*, Second Edition, edited by Alan Barnard and Jonathan Spencer (London and New York: Routledge, 2011).

CHAPTER 4. AUTOFICTION: *STAINED RADIANCE* AND *THE THIRTEENTH DISCIPLE*

1. The French critical theorist Serge Doubrovsky is credited with inventing the term 'autofiction' in 1977 with reference to his novel *Fils* (Paris: Galilée, 1977) as a self-explanatory concept representing the dynamic melding of autobiography and biography in which the author uses the detached modes of fiction to undertake a search for self.
2. Letter, Mitchell to Alexander Gray, dated 14 November 1930, NLS MS26109.
3. Mitchell's 'Synopsis of Memoirs of a Materialist', NLS MS26060 (*Sm*785), cites his second novel as an exemplar of the 'general line of treatment' pursued in his previous published works in relation to his 'early days'.
4. Letter, Mitchell to Alexander Gray, dated 14 November 1930, NLS MS26109.

CHAPTER 5. SETTING TALES UPON THE TRUTH: *THREE GO BACK*, *THE LOST TRUMPET* AND *GAY HUNTER*

1. Christopher Booker, *The Seven Basic Plots: Why We Tell Stories* (London: Continuum International Publishing Group Ltd, 2004), pp.69–106.

CHAPTER 6. HAUNTED BY HORRORS: *IMAGE AND SUPERSCRIPTION* AND *SPARTACUS*

1. Letter, Mitchell to Helen B Cruickshank, dated 18 November 1933, NLS MS26109.
2. Christopher Booker, *The Seven Basic Plots: Why We Tell Stories*, pp.193–214.

3. Barry Strauss has written the most vivid and convincing modern account of the Spartacus legend in *The Spartacus War* (London: Weidenfeld and Nicolson, 2009). Brent D Shaw has made the most useful compilation of the classical sources in *Spartacus and the Slave Wars: A Brief History with Documents* (London: Palgrave Macmillan, 2001). Strangely, he omits Mitchell's novel from his bibliography, which lists in the section on 'Spartacus in Fiction' only the later novels by Howard Fast (*Spartacus*, 1951) and Arthur Koestler (*The Gladiators*, 1939).

CHAPTER 7. DISTANT COUSIN LEWIS GRASSIC GIBBON: *A SCOTS QUAIR (SUNSET SONG, CLOUD HOWE* AND *GREY GRANITE)* AND *SCOTTISH SCENE*

1. The contract, signed by Jarrolds director HR Hale and by Mitchell, stipulates that Mitchell will tender to them 'the next three books which he shall write under the pseudonym of "Lewis Gibbon", which said three books shall be novels of not less than 80 000 words each in length' (NLS Acc.10966).
2. Mitchell's personal library is now housed at Edinburgh University Library Special Collections.
3. For the full cultural background to the Scottish literary revival in the twentieth century, see Margery Palmer McCulloch's defining study, *Scottish Modernism and Its Contexts 1918–1959: Literature, National Identity and Cultural Exchange* (Edinburgh: Edinburgh University Press, 2009) and her generous selection from these seminal publications in *Modernism and Nationalism: Literature and Society in Scotland 1918–1939* (Glasgow: Association for Scottish Literary Studies, 2004).
4. For a concise outline of the history of modern Scottish publishing, see Alistair McCleery, *The Porpoise Press 1922–39* (Edinburgh: Merchiston Publishing, 1988), Chapter 1.
5. A detailed comparison of the two novels is given in Douglas F Young, *Beyond the Sunset* (Aberdeen: Impulse Publications Limited, 1973), pp.146–53.
6. See William Donaldson, *Popular Literature in Victorian Scotland* (Aberdeen: Aberdeen University Press, 1986) and *The Language of the People: Scots Prose from the Victorian Revival*, edited by William Donaldson (Aberdeen: Aberdeen University Press, 1989).
7. Gibbon thus employs a particularly robust form of Michael Bakhtin's 'heteroglossic' narrative voice, creating multiple points of view that collectively, with careful aggregation of the evidence, hold out some kind of authorial truth. (See Michael M Bakhtin, *The Dialogic Imagination* [Austen and London: University of Texas Press, 1981].)

8. Cuthbert Graham, 'A Memory of Lewis Grassic Gibbon: Script of Talk on the Meldrum Transmitter', February 1960, NLS MS26097.
9. Letter, Ray Mitchell to the present writer, dated 1 May 1978.
10. Russian critic Svetlana Boym has made an illuminating distinction between what she terms 'restorative nostalgia', involving the censoring of the past into a 'perfect snapshot' of home and homeland purged of its blemishes, and bereft of the ironic and humorous detachment of the 'reflective nostalgia', used to fulfil a positive purpose – the latter of which perfectly defines Mitchell's mode of approach in *Sunset Song*. (Svetlana Boym, *The Future of Nostalgia* [New York: Basic Books, 2001], pp.41–56.)
11. A full record of this whole shameful episode in British military history is given in Julian Putkowski and Julian Sykes, *Shot at Dawn* (Barnsley: Pen and Sword Books, 2017), first published in 1989.
12. Lewis Grassic Gibbon, 'News of Battle: Queries for Mr. Whyte', *The Free Man*, 3 (17 March 1934), p.9.
13. Letter, Mitchell to Neil M Gunn, dated 2 November 1934, NLS Dep.209.
14. Mitchell, Notebook, NLS MS26041.
15. Letter, Mitchell to James Barke, dated 26 July 1933, in the Barke Archive in the Mitchell Library, Glasgow.
16. See Graham Robb, 'Introduction', in Honoré de Balzac, *Old Man Goriot*, translated by Olivia McCannon (London: Penguin Books Ltd, 2011), pp.xviii–xxix.
17. Mitchell, 'CURTAIN RAISER', NLS MS26040. Thomas Crawford has reproduced this as an appendix to the Canongate Classics edition of *Grey Granite* published in 1990, on pp.205–8.
18. See Maxim Gorky et al., *Soviet Writers' Congress 1934: The Debate on Socialist Realism and Modernism in the Soviet Union* (London: Lawrence and Wishart Ltd, 1977), first published in 1935.
19. See Peter Kingsford, *The Hunger Marchers in Britain 1920–1939* (London: Lawrence and Wishart Ltd, 1982).
20. See Max Adereth, 'What is *"Littérature Engagée"*?', *Commitment in Modern French Literature* (1967), republished in *Marxists on Literature*, edited by David Craig (Harmondsworth: Penguin, 1975), pp.445–85. The full significance of Aragon's term in relation to Mitchell as a writer of maverick radicalism who freely dedicates his writing to social and political ends, principally in *Image and Superscription*, *Spartacus* and *Grey Granite*, is expounded by the present author in *Lewis Grassic Gibbon: A Revolutionary Writer* (Edinburgh: Capercaillie Books, 2016), pp.22–3, 58, 63–4, 114.
21. An informed history of *Left Review* by David Margolies can be found in *Culture and Crisis in Britain in the 30s*, edited by Jon Clark et al. (London: Lawrence and Wishart, 1979), pp.67–82. Grassic

Gibbon's contribution is republished in the anthology *Writing the Revolution: Cultural Criticism from Left Review*, edited by David Margolies (London: Pluto Press, 1998), pp.38–9 (*Sm737–9*).

22. Among the most memorable Scottish profiles were those by George Malcolm Thomson (*The Re-Discovery of Scotland*, 1928; *Scotland: That Distressed Area*, 1935); Moray McLaren (*Return to Scotland: An Egoist's Journey*, 1930); William Power (*My Scotland*, 1934; *Scotland and the Scots*, 1934); George Blake (*The Heart of Scotland*, 1934); and Edwin Muir (*Scottish Journey*, 1935).

CHAPTER 8. LEGACY

1. The present writer's article 'The Exportation of Lewis Grassic Gibbon' published in *Scottish Literary Review*, 8 (Spring/Summer 2016), pp.93–109 provides a comprehensive critical analysis of the various stage, radio, television and film adaptations made of Mitchell's work.
2. William Power, *Literature and Oatmeal: What Literature Has Meant to Scotland* (London: George Routledge and Sons Ltd, 1935), pp.192–3. Full details of major criticism on Mitchell's work are listed under Further Reading, while a detailed inventory of secondary criticism, regularly updated, appears on the website of the Grassic Gibbon Centre, at www.grassicgibbon.com/critical-works/.
3. Kurt Wittig, *The Scottish Tradition in Literature* (Edinburgh: Oliver & Boyd, 1958), p.330.
4. Maurice Lindsay, *History of Scottish Literature* (London: Robert Hale, 1977), p.414.
5. Francis Russell Hart, *The Scottish Novel: A Critical Survey* (London: John Murray, 1978), pp. 229–41.
6. Trevor Royle, *The Macmillan Companion to Scottish Literature* (London: Macmillan, 1983), pp.216–7.
7. Alan Bold, *Modern Scottish Literature* (London: Longman, 1983), pp.123–39.
8. Roderick Watson, *The Literature of Scotland* (London: Macmillan, 1984), p.393.
9. Isobel Murray, 'Novelists of the Renaissance' and Manfred Malzahn, 'The Industrial Novel', *The History of Scottish Literature Volume 4*, edited by Cairns Craig (Aberdeen: AUP, 1987), pp.103–17 and pp.229–41, respectively.
10. Cairns Craig, *The Modern Scottish Novel: Narrative and the National Imagination* (Edinburgh: Edinburgh University Press, 1999), p.127.
11. Robert Crawford, *Scotland's Books: The Penguin History of Scottish Literature* (London: Penguin Books, 2007), pp.558–62.

12. Gerard Carruthers, *Scottish Literature (Edinburgh Critical Guides)* (Edinburgh: Edinburgh University Press, 2009), p.66.
13. Scott Lyall, 'Hugh MacDiarmid and the Scottish Renaissance', *The Cambridge Companion to Scottish Literature*, edited by Gerard Carruthers and Liam McIlvanney (Cambridge: Cambridge University Press, 2012), pp.173–87.
14. The most rigorous Marxist analyses of Gibbon's achievement following James Barke's 'Lewis Grassic Gibbon', *Left Review*, 2 (February 1936), pp.220–5, are Ian Milner's 'An Estimation of Lewis Grassic Gibbon's *A Scots Quair*', *Marxist Quarterly*, 1 (October 1954), pp.207–18 and Jack Mitchell's 'The Struggle for the Working-Class Novel in Scotland, 1900–39', *Zeitschrift fur Anglistik und Amerikanistik*, 21 (1973), pp.396–403.
15. See JKA Thomaneck, '*A Scots Quair* in East Germany', *Scottish Literary Journal*, 3 (July 1976), pp.62–6 and Ian Campbell, 'Gibbon and MacDiarmid in the German Democratic Republic', *Books in Scotland*, no.6 (Winter 1979–80), pp.6–7.
16. *The International Companion to Lewis Grassic Gibbon* (Glasgow: Scottish Literature International, 2015), edited by Scott Lyall, gathers together essays by scholars from home and abroad in order to demonstrate Gibbon's continuing relevance 'both in Scotland and internationally'.
17. Ian S Munro, *Leslie Mitchell: Lewis Grassic Gibbon* (Edinburgh: Oliver & Boyd Ltd), p.216.
18. Letter, Mitchell to Compton Mackenzie, dated 19 September 1932, Harry Ransom Humanities Research Center, University of Texas at Austin.
19. Lewis Grassic Gibbon, 'The Antique Scene', *Sm*, pp.17–21; Alasdair Gray, *Of Me and Others* (Glasgow: Cargo Publishing (UK) Ltd, 2014), p.2.
20. Adrian Poole, 'Introduction', *The Cambridge Companion to English Novelists*, edited by Adrian Poole (Cambridge: Cambridge University Press, 2009), p.9.
21. Arnold Kettle, *An Introduction to the English Novel, Volume 2* (London: Hutchinson University Library, 1953), p.65.
22. Raymond Williams, *The Country and the City* (London and New York: Oxford University Press, 1973), p.271.
23. H Gustav Klaus, 'Socialist Fiction in the 1930s: Some Preliminary Observations', *The 1930s: A Challenge to Orthodoxy*, edited by John Lucas (Hassocks: Harvester, 1978), p.32.
24. David Smith, *Socialist Propaganda in the Twentieth-Century British Novel* (London: Macmillan, 1978); Valentine Cunningham, *British Writers of the Thirties* (Oxford: Oxford University Press, 1988); Andy Croft, *Red Letter Days: British Fiction in the 1930s* (London: Lawrence

and Wishart, 1990); Ian Haywood, *Working-Class Fiction: From Chartism to Trainspotting* (Plymouth: Northcote House, 1997); James Smith (editor), *The Cambridge Companion to British Literature of the 1930s* (Cambridge: Cambridge University Press, 2019).

25. See in particular Deirdre Burton, 'A Feminist Reading of Lewis Grassic Gibbon's *A Scots Quair*', *The British Working-Class Novel in the Twentieth Century*, edited by Jeremy Hawthorn (London: Edward Arnold, 1984), pp.35–46; Alison Lumsden, '"Women's Time": Reading the *Quair* as a Feminist Text', *A Flame in the Mearns: Lewis Grassic Gibbon: A Centenary Celebration*, edited by Margery Palmer McCulloch and Sarah M Dunnigan (Glasgow: Association for Scottish Literary Studies Occasional Papers Number 13, ASLS, 2003), pp.41–53; and Glenda Norquay, 'Lewis Grassic Gibbon and Women', *The International Companion to Lewis Grassic Gibbon*, edited by Scott Lyall, op.cit., pp.76–88.

26. See in particular Douglas S Mack, *Scottish Fiction and the British Empire* (Edinburgh: Edinburgh University Press, 2006), pp.206–13; and Scott Lyall, '"East is West and West is East": Lewis Grassic Gibbon's Quest for Ultimate Cosmopolitanism', *Scottish Literature and Postcolonial Literature: Comparative Texts and Critical Perspectives*, edited by Michael Gardiner, Graeme MacDonald and Niall O'Gallagher (Edinburgh: EUP, 2011), pp.136–46.

27. See Margery Palmer McCulloch, 'Modernism and Marxism in *A Scots Quair*', *A Flame in the Mearns: Lewis Grassic Gibbon: A Centenary Celebration*, op.cit., pp.27–40 and *Scottish Modernism and Its Contexts 1918–1959: Literature, National Identity and Cultural Exchange*, pp.131–44; Scott Lyall, 'On Cosmopolitanism and Late Style: Lewis Grassic Gibbon and James Joyce', *Scottish and International Modernisms: Relationships and Reconfigurations*, edited by Emma Dymock and Margery Palmer McCulloch (Glasgow: ASLS, 2011), pp.101–15; and Morag Shiach, 'Lewis Grassic Gibbon and Modernism', *The International Companion to Lewis Grassic Gibbon*, edited by Scott Lyall, op.cit., pp.9–21.

28. The timely volume of essays *Ecology and the Literature of the British Left: The Red and the Green*, edited by John Rignall and H Gustav Klaus with Valentine Cunningham (London and New York: Routledge, 2016 [2012]), traces the confluence of an 'environmental sensibility' and 'a leftist position' pertaining from the Romantic period, taking in the radical environmentalism of William Morris and HG Wells as well as James Barke and Grassic Gibbon.

29. Timothy Clark, *The Value of Ecocriticism* (Cambridge: Cambridge University Press, 2019), pp.3–4.

Bibliography

Books by James Leslie Mitchell and Lewis Grassic Gibbon

(Unless stated otherwise, books were published under Mitchell's own name.)

Hanno: or The Future of Exploration (London: Kegan Paul, Trench Trubner and Co. Ltd, 1928).
Stained Radiance: A Fictionist's Prelude (London: Jarrolds, 1930).
The Thirteenth Disciple: Being Portrait and Saga of Malcom Maudslay in his Adventure Through the Dark Corridor (London: Jarrolds, 1931).
The Calends of Cairo, Introduced by Mr. H.G. Wells and Dr. Leonard Huxley (London: Jarrolds, 1931). (Published as *Cairo Dawns: A Story Cycle with a Proem* [Indianapolis: the Bobbs-Merrill Company, 1931].)
Three Go Back (London: Jarrolds, 1932).
The Lost Trumpet (London: Jarrolds, 1932).
Lewis Grassic Gibbon, *Sunset Song: A Novel* (London: Jarrolds, 1932).
Persian Dawns, Egyptian Nights, with a Foreword by J.D. Beresford (London: Jarrolds, 1932).
Image and Superscription: A Novel (London: Jarrolds, 1933).
Lewis Grassic Gibbon, *Cloud Howe* (London: Jarrolds, 1933).
Spartacus (London: Jarrolds, 1933).
Lewis Grassic Gibbon, *Niger: The Life of Mungo Park* (Edinburgh: The Porpoise Press/London: Faber and Faber, 1934).
The Conquest of the Maya, with a Foreword by Professor G. Elliot Smith (London: Jarrolds, 1934).
Gay Hunter (London: William Heinemann, 1934).
Hugh MacDiarmid and Lewis Grassic Gibbon, *Scottish Scene: or The Intelligent Man's Guide to Albyn* (London: Jarrolds, 1934).
J. Leslie Mitchell and Lewis Grassic Gibbon, *Nine Against the Unknown: A Record of Geographical Exploration* (London: Jarrolds, 1934). (Published under sole authorship of Mitchell as *Earth Conquerors: The Lives and Achievements of the Great Explorers* [New York: Simon and Schuster Inc., 1934].)

Lewis Grassic Gibbon, *Grey Granite* (London: Jarrolds, 1934).
Lewis Grassic Gibbon, *A Scots Quair* [comprising *Sunset Song*, *Cloud Howe* and *Grey Granite*] (London: Jarrolds, 1946).
Lewis Grassic Gibbon, *A Scots Hairst: Essays and Short Stories* [including juvenilia and poetry], edited by Ian S. Munro (London: Hutchinson, 1967).
Lewis Grassic Gibbon, *The Speak of the Mearns* (Edinburgh: The Ramsay Head Press, 1982).
Lewis Grassic Gibbon, *Smeddum: A Lewis Grassic Gibbon Anthology*, edited by Valentina Bold (Edinburgh: Canongate Books, 2001).

Non-fiction Articles

'The End of the Maya Old Empire', *Antiquity*, 4 (September 1930), pp.285–302.
'Yucatan: New Empire Tribes and Culture Waves', *Antiquity*, 4 (December 1930), pp.438–52.
'The Diffusionist Heresy', *The Twentieth Century*, 1 (March 1931), pp.14–18.
'Inka and pre-Inka', *Antiquity*, 5 (June 1931), pp.172–84.
Review of Julio C. Tello, *Antiguo Peru: primera epoca*, *Antiquity*, 5 (June 1931), p.257.
Review of Hiram Bingham, *Machu Picchu: A Citadel of the Incas*, *Antiquity*, 5 (June 1931), pp.263–4.
'Grafton Elliot Smith: Anthropologist, Historian, Humanist', *The Millgate Monthly*, 26 (July 1931), pp.578–82.
Review of P.A. Means, *Ancient Civilizations of the Andes*, *Antiquity*, 5 (September 1931), pp.391–2.
'The Prince's Placenta and Prometheus as God', *The Twentieth Century*, 2 (February 1932), pp.16–18.
'William James Perry: A Revolutionary Anthropologist', *The Millgate Monthly*, 27 (March 1932), pp.323–6.
'The Buddha of America', *The Cornhill Magazine*, 72 (May 1932), pp.595–604.
Lewis Grassic Gibbon, 'Sunset Song: Author's Reply to the Editor', *The Fife Herald and Journal*, 28 September 1932, p.2.
'Introduction', Heinrich Mann, *The Blue Angel* (London: Jarrolds, 1932), pp.5–7.
'Introduction', Peter Freuchen, *Eskimo: A Novel* (London: Jarrolds, 1932), pp.5–7.
Louis Katin, 'Author of Sunset Song', *The Evening News* (Glasgow), 16 February 1933, p.6 is based upon an interview conducted at his home in Welwyn Garden City, Hertfordshire.

Lewis Grassic Gibbon, 'Book Reviews: Fiction. Scots Novels of the Half-Year', *The Free Man*, 2 (24 June 1933), p.7.
'Ancient Mexico', *Antiquity*, 7 (September 1933), pp.311–23.
'Grieve – Scotsman', *The Free Man*, 2 (9 September 1933), p.7.
'Book Review – Man and the Universe', *The Free Man*, 2 (7 October 1933), p.9.
Lewis Grassic Gibbon, 'Book Review – In Oor Kailyaird', *The Free Man*, 2 (7 October 1933), p.9.
Lewis Grassic Gibbon, 'A Note the Reader is Advised to Read' and 'Glossary', *Sunset Song* (The Century Co.: New York, 1933), p.vii and pp.303–6.
Lewis Grassic Gibbon, 'A Novelist Looks at the Cinema', *Cinema Quarterly*, 3 (1935), pp.81–5.
Lewis Grassic Gibbon, '"Canting Humbug": To the Editor of "The Mearns Leader"', *The Mearns Leader and Kincardineshire Mail*, 8 February 1934, p.1.
Lewis Grassic Gibbon, 'New Novels: Mr. Barke and Others', *The Free Man*, 3 (24 February 1934), p.6.
Lewis Grassic Gibbon, '"I Kent his Faither!": A Scots Writer Reviews his Reviewers', *Glasgow Evening News* (Saturday Supplement), 24 February 1934, p.1.
Lewis Grassic Gibbon, 'News of Battle: Queries for Mr. Whyte', *The Free Man*, 3 (17 March 1934), p.9.
Lewis Grassic Gibbon, 'Controversy: Writers' International (British Section)', *Left Review*, 1 (February 1935), pp.179–80.
'Religions of Ancient Mexico', *Religions: The Journal of Transactions of the Society for Promoting the Study of Religions*, no.13 (October 1935), pp.11–20.

Short Stories

'Siva Plays the Game', *T.P.'s and Cassell's Weekly*, 18 October 1924, pp.849–50. (Reprinted in *The Millgate Monthly*, 26 [April 1931], pp.405–7; revised and reprinted as 'Siwa Plays the Game', *PDEN* pp.259–77.)
'If You Sleep in the Moonlight', *Grim Death*, edited by Christine Campbell Thomson (London: Selwyn and Blount, 1928), pp.11–18. (Revised and reprinted in *Reynolds's Illustrated News*, 15 March 1931, p.10.)
'For Ten's Sake', *The Cornhill Magazine*, 66 (January 1929), pp.38–51. (Revised and reprinted in *CC* pp.13–33.)
'One Man with a Dream', *The Cornhill Magazine*, 66 (May 1929), pp.589–600. (Revised and reprinted as 'Revolt' in *PDEN* pp.180–99.)

'He Who Seeks', *The Cornhill Magazine*, 67 (July 1929), pp.97–107. (Revised and reprinted in *CC* pp.37–53.)

'The Epic', *The Cornhill Magazine*, 67 (August 1929), pp.160–70. (Revised and reprinted in *CC* pp.92–108.)

'The Road', *The Cornhill Magazine*, 67 (September 1929), pp.341–52. (Revised and reprinted as 'The Lost Prophetess' in *CC* pp.54–72.)

'A Volcano in the Moon', *The Cornhill Magazine*, 67 (October 1929), pp.463–76. (Revised and reprinted in *CC* pp.109–30.)

'The Life and Death of Elia Constantinides', *The Cornhill Magazine*, 67 (November 1929), pp.513–26. (Revised and reprinted in *CC* pp.131–52.)

'Cockcrow', *The Cornhill Magazine*, 67 (December 1929), pp.641–54. (Revised and reprinted in *CC* pp.153–73.)

'Gift of the River', *The Cornhill Magazine*, 68 (January 1930), pp.17–30. (Revised and reprinted in *CC* pp.218–38.)

'East is West', *The Cornhill Magazine*, 68 (February 1930), pp.129–43. (Revised and reprinted in *CC* pp.195–217.)

'Vernal', *The Cornhill Magazine*, 68 (March 1930), pp.257–70. (Revised and reprinted in *CC* pp.174–94.)

'Daybreak', *The Cornhill Magazine*, 68 (April 1930), pp.385–96. (Revised and reprinted in *CC* pp.73–91.)

'It is Written', *The Cornhill Magazine*, 68 (May 1930), pp.513–26. (Revised and reprinted in *CC* pp.239–60.)

'The Passage of the Dawn', *The Cornhill Magazine*, 68 (June 1930), pp.641–55. (Revised and reprinted in *CC* pp.261–82.)

'The Refugees', *John O' London's Weekly*, 25 (11 April 1931), pp.5–7. (Reprinted in *The Millgate Monthly*, 27 [October 1931], pp.33–8; revised and reprinted as 'Amber in Cold Sea', in *PDEN* pp.161–79.)

'Roads to Freedom', *The Millgate Monthly*, 26 (June 1931), pp.547–50. (Reprinted as 'The Road to Freedom', in *Masterpiece of Thrills*, edited by R Huson [London: A Daily Express Publication, n.d. (1936)], pp. 463–71.)

'Near Farnboru: A Nightmare Vision of the Future', *Reynolds's Illustrated News*, 12 July 1931, pp.10, 18. (Reprinted under authorship of Lewis Grassic Gibbon as 'First and Last Woman', in *Masterpiece of Thrills*, pp. 729–35.)

'A Footnote to History', *The Cornhill Magazine*, 71 (August 1931), pp.195–212. (Revised and reprinted as 'The Lovers' in *PDEN* pp.33–62.)

'The Lost Constituent', *The Cornhill Magazine*, 71 (September 1931), pp.355–64. (Revised and reprinted in *PDEN* pp.17–32.)

'A Stele from Atlantis', *Reynolds's Illustrated News*, 20 September 1931, p.10. (Reprinted under authorship of Lewis Grassic Gibbon, in *Masterpiece of Thrills*, pp.271–6.)

'The Floods of Spring', *The Cornhill Magazine*, 71 (November 1931), pp.623–38. (Revised and reprinted in *PDEN* pp.63–89.)

'Thermopylae', *The Cornhill Magazine*, 71 (December 1931), pp.684–703. (Revised and reprinted as 'Dienekes' Dream' in *PDEN* pp.225–58.)

'O Mistress Mine!', *The Millgate Monthly*, 27 (May 1932), pp.491–4.

'Lost Tribes', *Reynolds's Illustrated News*, 19 June 1932, p.10. (Reprinted as 'Lost Tribe', in *The Millgate Monthly*, 29 [January 1934], pp.199–202 and as 'Lost Tribes', *Masterpiece of Thrills*, pp.623–30.)

'The Last Ogre', *The Cornhill Magazine*, 72 (June 1932), pp.699–711. (Revised and reprinted in *PDEN* pp.90–110.)

'Cartaphilus', *The Cornhill Magazine*, 73 (September 1932), pp.344–57. (Revised and reprinted in *PDEN* pp.111–34.)

'Camelia Comes to Cairo', *PDEN* pp.200–24.

'The Children of Ceres', *PDEN* pp.278–86.

Lewis Grassic Gibbon, 'Greenden', *The Scots Magazine*, 18 (December 1932), pp.168–76. (Revised and reprinted in *ScSc* pp.69–79.)

Lewis Grassic Gibbon, 'Smeddum', *The Scots Magazine*, 18 (January 1933), pp.248–56. (Revised and reprinted in *ScSc* pp.117–27.)

Lewis Grassic Gibbon, 'Clay', *The Scots Magazine*, 18 (February 1933), pp.329–39. (Revised and reprinted in *ScSc* pp.268–79.)

'Dawn in Alarlu', *The Cornhill Magazine*, 74 (February 1933), pp.185–97. (Revised and reprinted in *PDEN* pp.135–57.)

Lewis Grassic Gibbon, 'Sim', *The Free Man*, 2 (10 June 1933), pp.5–7. (Revised and reprinted in *ScSc* pp.215–25.)

Lewis Grassic Gibbon, 'Forsaken', *ScSc* pp.178–88.

'Busman's Holiday', *Masterpiece of Thrills*, pp.37–52.

J. Leslie Mitchell and Fytton Armstrong, 'Kametis and Evelpis', *Masterpiece of Thrills*, pp.193–238.

Lewis Grassic Gibbon, 'The Woman of Leadenhall Street', *Masterpiece of Thrills*, pp.567–86.

Further Reading

Books on Mitchell/Gibbon

Campbell, Ian, *Lewis Grassic Gibbon* (Edinburgh: Scottish Academic Press, 1985).

Ehland, Christoph, *Picaresque Perspectives – Exiled Identities: A Structural and Methodological Analysis of the Picaresque as a Literary Archetype in the Works of James Leslie Mitchell* (Heidelberg: Universitatsverlag Winter Heidelberg, 2003).

Geddes, Clarke, *Nemesis in the Mearns* (Edinburgh: Scottish Cultural Press, 1996).

Gifford, Douglas, *Neil M Gunn & Lewis Grassic Gibbon* (Edinburgh: Oliver & Boyd, 1983).

Lyall, Scott, editor, *The International Companion to Lewis Grassic Gibbon* (Glasgow: Scottish Literature International, 2015).

McCulloch, Margery Palmer, and Dunnigan, Sarah M, editors, *A Flame in the Mearns: Lewis Grassic Gibbon: A Centenary Celebration* (Glasgow: Association for Scottish Literary Studies Occasional Papers Number 13, ASLS, 2003).

Malcolm, William K, *A Blasphemer & Reformer: A Study of James Leslie Mitchell/Lewis Grassic Gibbon* (Aberdeen: Aberdeen University Press, 1984).

Malcolm, William K, *Lewis Grassic Gibbon: A Revolutionary Writer* (Edinburgh: Capercaillie Books, 2016).

Munro, Ian S, *Leslie Mitchell: Lewis Grassic Gibbon* (Edinburgh: Oliver & Boyd, 1966).

Whitfield, Peter, *Grassic Gibbon and his World* (Aberdeen: Aberdeen Journals Ltd, 1994).

Young, Douglas F, *Beyond the Sunset: A Study of James Leslie Mitchell (Lewis Grassic Gibbon)* (Aberdeen: Impulse Publications, 1973).

Zagratzki, Uwe, *Libertare und Utopische Tendenzen im Erzahlwerk James Leslie Mitchells (Lewis Grassic Gibbons)* (Frankfurt am Main: Peter Lang, 1991).

Selected Essays on Mitchell/Gibbon

(Full details of critical works on Mitchell are contained in the regularly updated bibliography on the Grassic Gibbon Centre's website, at www.grassicgibbon.com/critical-works/.)

Barke, James, 'Lewis Grassic Gibbon', *Left Review*, 2 (February 1936), pp.220–5.

Burton, Deirdre, 'A Feminist Reading of Lewis Grassic Gibbon's *A Scots Quair*', *The British Working-Class Novel in the Twentieth Century*, edited by Jeremy Hawthorn (London: Edward Arnold, 1984), pp.35–46.

Cruickshank, Helen B, *Octobiography* (Montrose: The Standard Press, 1976), pp.87–92.

Grieve, CM, 'Contemporary Scottish Studies, I: Lewis Grassic Gibbon', *The Free Man*, 2 (29 July 1933), p.7.

Gunn, Neil M, 'Nationalism in Writing: Tradition and Magic in the Work of Lewis Grassic Gibbon', *The Scots Magazine*, 30 (October 1938), pp.28–35.

Mitchell, Jack, 'The Struggle for the Working-Class Novel in Scotland, 1900–39', *Zeitschrift fur Anglistik und Amerikanistik*, 21 (1973), pp.396–403.

Muir, Edwin, 'Lewis Grassic Gibbon (J Leslie Mitchell): An Appreciation', *Scottish Standard*, March 1935, pp.23–4.

Index

Aberdeen 8, 9, 10, 11, 62, 81, 82, 87, 98, 101, 122, 129
Aberdeen Daily Journal 9, 11
Aberdeen Soviet 10, 122
Aberdeen Trades Council 10
Aberdeenshire 4, 7, 39, 40
absurdism 107
Adereth, Max 102n20
Africa 13, 33
Alabama (USA) 106
Aldred, Guy 10, 11
Alexander, William
  The Authentic History of Peter Grundie 75
  Johnny Gibb of Gushetneuk 75
  The Laird of Drammochdyle 75
Alexandria (Egypt) 19
Allan, Dot
  Hunger March 102, 134
America 20, 54, 63
  see also United States (USA)
Amundsen, Roald 30
anarchist theory 67, 122
  see also anarchism 29
Anarchocommunist Party 10
Angles 124
Angus 121
Angus, Marion 105
anti-fascist 54, 103
Antiquity 29
Appian 63
Appian Way (Rome) 64
Arabian Fantasy 18

Arabs and Jews, conflict between 12
Aragon, Louis 102
Aramaic 119
Arbuthnott (Aberdeenshire) 13, 27, 73, 80, 81, 82, 88, 94, 96, 115, 120
Arbuthott Church of St Ternan 80
Arbuthnott Estates 8, 8n10
  see also Arbuthnott Estate 7n5, 8n8
Arbuthnott Kirkyard 15
Arbuthnott School 5, 25, 32, 43
Argyll 63
Asia 13
Atlantis 50
Auchenblae (Aberdeenshire) 80
Auchterless (Aberdeenshire) 7, 8, 79, 95, 96, 115
the Auden Generation 103

Baghdad (Iraq) 12, 13
Bahaira (Beheira) (Egypt) 21
Bahamas 27
Bakhtin, Michael M
  The Dialogic Imagination 76n7
the Balfour Declaration 12
Balwearie (Fife) 80
Balzac, Honoré de
  La Comedie Humaine 92
Banchory (Aberdeenshire) 4
Barke, James 89, 102, 134
  Major Operation 134

INDEX

the Barmekin (Aberdeenshire) 108, 109
Barnard, Alan and Spencer, Jonathan
  The Routledge Encyclopaedia of Social and Cultural Anthropology (editors) 35n4
Barrie, JM 90
Basra (Iraq) 13
Battle of Culloden 124
Battle of Flodden 82, 124
Baxter, Harold and Jean 72
BBC Home Service 129
BBC1 'Play for Today' 129
BBC radio 129
BBC Scotland (television) 129
Beckett, Samuel 107
Bennet, Arnold 18, 119
Bering, Vitus 36
Bervie (Aberdeenshire) 80, 94, 95, 96
  see also Inverbervie 94, 95, 96, 114, 130
Bervie Water 80, 112
the Bible 124
Blair, Tony 123
Blake, George 89
  The Heart of Scotland 111n22
Bloody Friday (Glasgow) 11
Bloomfield (Arbuthnott) 8, 32, 80, 94
Bold, Alan
  Modern Scottish Literature 132
Booker, Christopher
  The Seven Basic Plots: Why We Tell Stories 50n1, 60n2
the Borders (Scotland) 31
Borges, Jorge Luis 18
Boym, Svetlana
  The Future of Nostalgia 83n10
Brendon, Piers
  The Decline and Fall of the British Empire 1781–1997 21n2
Bridie, James 89
Brierley, Walter
  Means-Test Man 102, 134

Britain 5, 7, 10, 12, 13, 17, 70, 134, 136
  see also Great Britain 104
British colonialism 33
  see also British imperialism 13
  see also spirit of empire 12
British control in Egypt 13
British forces in Iraq 13
British Library 25
  see also British Museum 64
British National Party (BNP) 135
British Socialist Party (BSP) 10
Brown, George Douglas
  The House with the Green Shutters 34, 88, 90, 116
Buchan (Scots dialect) 75
Buddha 42
Bulaq Bridge (Cairo) 20
Bulloch, JM 72
Burns, Robert 1, 3, 70, 74, 127
Burton, Deirdre 138n25
Burton, Richard 36
Butterfield, Herbert 28

Caesar, Julius 52, 62
Cairene Labour Union 22, 54
Cairn o' Mount (Aberdeenshire) 121
Cairo (Egypt) 13, 19, 20, 21, 22, 53, 54
Calabria (Italy) 64
Calvinism 80
Camlachie (Glasgow) 11
Campbell, Ian 130, 135n15
Camus, Albert 67, 107
Canada 4, 8, 114
capitalism 104
  see also neoliberal capitalism 106, 135
Capua (Italy) 64
Carruthers, Gerard
  Critical Guide to Scottish Literature 133
  with McIlvanney, Liam, *The Cambridge Companion to Scottish Literature* (editor) 133

Carswell, Donald and Catherine 72, 89
Carter, Howard 20
Carter, Ian
  Farm Life in Northeast Scotland 1840–1914 3n2
Carthage (Tunisia) 65
Celts (Kelts) 124
Central America 34, 43, 44, 48, 132
central belt (Scotland) 10
Chatham (Kent) 60
Chiang Kai-shek 58
the Chilterns (southeast England) 55
Christ 42, 68, 97, 113, 117, 118, 119
Christian socialism 97
Christianity 2
Church of Scotland 124
the Citadel (Cairo) 20
the Citadel Hospital 20
Civil List Pension 128
Clark, Timothy 139
  The Value of Ecocriticism 139n29
the Cold War 135
Coleridge, ST 110
Columbus, Christopher 27, 36
communism 29, 90, 91, 102
Communist International (Comintern) 10
Communist Party (CP) 41, 104, 109
Communist Party of Great Britain (CPGB) 3, 11, 102, 103
communist theory 29, 67
Conservatives 95, 123
Continental Hotel (Cairo) 19
Cording, Alastair 129
The Cornhill Magazine 14, 19
Craig, Cairns
  The History of Scottish Literature 132
  The Modern Scottish Novel 133
Craig, David
  Marxists on Literature (editor) 102n20

Crawford, Robert
  Scotland's Books 133
creationism 61
Croft, Andy
  Red Letter Days: British Fiction in the 1930s 138
Crofting 115
  see also Crofter(s) 1, 6, 80, 92
Cronin, AJ
  Hatter's Castle 34, 70, 116
Cruickshank, Helen B 59, 89
Cults (Aberdeen) 10
Cunningham, Valentine
  British Writers of the Thirties 138
Darien Scheme 124
Darwin, Charles 61
Davies, Terence
  Sunset Song (film) 129
Delville Wood (France) 46
Denmark 134
Dickens, Charles
  Great Expectations 75
  Hard Times 134
Diffusionism 28, 29, 35, 36, 43, 48, 51, 52, 54, 58, 61, 123, 124, 130, 131, 132
Donaldson, William
  The Language of the People: Scots Prose from the Victorian Revival (editor) 75n6
  Popular Literature in Victorian Scotland 75n6
Doric (Scots) 75
Doubrovsky, Serge 39n1
Douglas, Kirk 128
Douglasism 102
  see also Douglasites 106
Drumlithie (Aberdeenshire) 80
Drumtochty (Aberdeenshire) 99
  see also Glen of Drumtochty 73, 121
Dundee 8, 10
Dunn, JW 55
Dunnottar Castle (Aberdeenshire) 85

Echt (Aberdeenshire) 99, 100, 110
ecocriticism 139
Edelman, Marc 5n4
Edinburgh 30, 72, 98, 127
Edwardian age 2
  see also post-Victorian Britain 1
Egypt 12, 13, 19, 21, 22, 23, 53
  see also Ancient Egypt 35
Egyptian independence 13
Egyptian Wafd Party 23
Ehland, Christoph 130
Einstein, Albert 30, 58
Eliot, TS 28
Elliot, Jean 81
England 13, 20, 44, 53, 56, 89, 105, 134, 136
Ericsson, Leif 27, 36
Eskimo (Inuit) 27
Europe 9, 10, 11, 20, 30, 90, 106, 118, 134, 136
existentialism 107

Faber and Faber (publisher) 30
Fanon, Frantz 124
fascism 3, 49, 56, 90, 95, 102, 104
  see also Fascist Party 124
Fast, Howard 64, 128
  Spartacus 63n3
Faulkner, William 78
  As I Lay Dying 79
Fergusson, Niall
  Empire: How Britain Made the Modern World 21n2
Fife 10, 80
First World War 3, 9, 18, 47, 64, 74, 77, 79, 81, 86, 107, 123, 138
  see also Armistice Day 82
  see also battles in Northern France 46
  see also British Army Act 88
  see also the Western Front 51
Fisk, Robert
  The Great War for Civilization: The Conquest of the Middle East 21n2

Fitzgerald, Edward, *The Rubáiyát of Omar Khayyám* 18
Flaubert, Gustav
  Salammbô 65
Flecker, James Elroy, *The King of Alsander* 18
'The Flowers of the Forest' 81, 86
France 12, 13, 51, 53, 136
France, Anatole 18, 47
The Free Man 90, 111, 116
French Foreign Legion 62
French Revolution 84
Frenssen, Gustav
  Jörn Uhl 73
Freud, Sigmund 39

Gaelic literature 131
Galicia (Spain) 136
the Gallowgate (Aberdeen) 10
Galsworthy, John 18
Galt, John 74
Gamaijeh bazaar (Cairo) 20
Garnethill (Glasgow) 11
Geddes, Clarke 130
General Strike 14, 42, 47, 64, 79, 93, 95, 123
George Square (Glasgow) 11
Germany 10, 20, 51, 53, 64, 105, 124, 136
  see also East Germany 134
Gibbon, George (brother) 4
Gibbon, George (grandfather) 4
Gibbon, Lewis Grassic
  articles
    '"I Kent His Faither!": A Scots Writer Reviews His Reviewers' 31n3
    'News of Battle: Queries for Mr. Whyte' 90n12
  non-fiction books
    The Voice of Scotland series (editor) 90, 111, 131
    Niger 25, 30–4, 36, 74
    A Scots Hairst 128

INDEX

Scottish Scene (miscellany with MacDiarmid, Hugh) 5, 74, 75, 95, 111–25, 128
  conception 112
  cultural context 111
  'Aberdeen' 10, 98, 119, 121, 122–3
  'The Antique Scene' 120, 123, 124–5
  'Glasgow' 11, 119, 120, 121–2
  'The Land' 5–6, 69, 119, 120–1, 139
  'Literary Lights' 74, 75, 99, 120, 125
  'Religion' 120, 123–4
  'The Wrecker' 95, 120, 123
novels
  A Scots Quair 1, 30, 37, 69–111, 127, 128, 129, 130, 131, 132, 134, 136, 138, 139, 140
    anti-war theme 86–8
    as ecofiction 33, 139
    conception 69–74, 90–2, 98–100
    cultural context 70–4, 88–90, 90
    structure 79–80, 83–5, 101–2
  Sunset Song 1, 7, 14, 15, 27, 33, 35, 46, 52, 56, 57, 60, 69–90, 91, 92, 100–1, 107, 111, 112, 120, 128, 129, 130, 132, 137, 140
  see also American edition of *Sunset Song* 75, 84
  Cloud Howe 14, 42, 56, 64, 79, 90–7, 101, 107, 117, 123, 129, 130
  Grey Granite 41, 42, 79, 91, 96, 97, 98–111, 117, 118, 119, 129, 131, 132, 133, 134, 135
  The Speak of the Mearns 72
stories
  'Clay' 114–5, 129
  'Forsaken' 116–9
  'Greenden' 112–3, 114, 129

'Sim' 116, 129
'Smeddum' 113–4, 129
see also Mitchell, James Leslie
Gibbon, Lilias (Lily) Grant (mother) 3, 4, 15
see also Mitchell, Lily 80
Gibbon, Lilias Grassick (grandmother) 15, 73
Gifford, Douglas 130
Ginchy (France) 46
Giza (Egypt) 19
Gladkov, Fyodor
  Cement 99
Glasgow 10, 11, 39, 43, 45, 63, 73, 82, 101, 113, 122
Glasgow Communist Group 11
the Golden Age 51
the Gorbals (Glasgow) 11
Gorky, Maxim 54
  Mother 98, 134
Govan (Glasgow) 11
Graham, Cuthbert 78n8
Grampian Hills (Aberdeenshire) 112
Grassic Gibbon Centre 128
Gray, Alasdair
  Of Me and Others 137n19
Gray, Alexander 5, 34, 39, 46, 72
the Great Depression 95
Greece 20
Greenland 37
Greenwood, Walter
  Love on the Dole 102, 134
Grieve, Christopher Murray 71, 72, 73, 89, 112
see also MacDiarmid, Hugh
Guanahani (Bahamas) 27
Guestrow (Aberdeen) 10
Guha, Ranajit 7n6
Gulf of Mexico 60
Gunn, Neil 89, 90, 130, 131, 132

Haeckel, Ernst 46
Hale, Robert 70, 121
Hammersmith (London) 73
Hanno the Navigator 30

INDEX

Hardy, Thomas 132
Hart, Francis Russell
   The Scottish Novel 131
Harvest Home 81
Hay, J MacDougall
   Gillespie 34
Haywood, Ian
   Working-Class Fiction: From Chartism to Trainspotting 138
Heilbron, Vivien 129
Heimatkunst (regionalism) 73
Heliopolis (Cairo) 20
Heraclitus of Ephesus 57, 110
Highlands of Scotland 6
Hillhead of Seggat (Auchterless) 7
Hindu 35
Hitler, Adolf 58
Hogg, James 3, 74
Holstein, Duchy of 73
the Holy Land 12
Hungary 134
Hutchinson (publisher) 128
Huxley, Aldous
   Brave New World 55, 58
Huxley, Leonard 14, 19
Huxley, Thomas Henry 46

Ibn Saud 23
Incas 29
Independent Labour Party (ILP) 10
India 132
individualism 2
Insch (Aberdeenshire) 4
'The Internationale' 42, 106
Internationalism 122
Iraq 12, 13
   see also Mesopotamia 12
Ireland 10
Italian Renaissance 105
Italy 53, 64, 124, 134, 136

Jacobite rebellions (Scotland) 124
James I, King of Scotland
   The Kingis Quair 70

Japan 136
Jarrolds (publisher) 70, 91
   see also Jackdaw paperbacks 127
Jericho (Palestine) 53
Jerusalem (Israel) 12, 54
Jews 118
   see also anti-semitism 118
Jones, Lewis
   Cwmardy 102, 134
Joyce, James 41, 74, 77, 100, 125, 136
   Ulysses 18
Judas Iscariot 43

Kafka, Franz 107
Kailyard tradition 71, 88, 90, 132
Keats, John 127
Kelman, James 75, 133
Kenefick, William
   Red Scotland! The Rise and Fall of the Radical Left, c.1872 to 1932 10n11
Kentucky (USA) 63
Kettle, Arnold
   An Introduction to the English Novel, Volume 2 137
Khal Khalil (Khan al-Khalili) (Cairo) 20
Khedive (Egypt) 13, 21
Kildrummy (Aberdeenshire) 4
Kincardine 80
Kincardineshire 8, 9, 73, 98
King Street (Aberdeen) 8
Kingsford, Peter
   The Hunger Marchers in Britain 1920–1939 102n19
Kinneff (Aberdeenshire) 80, 98, 112, 114
Kipling, Rudyard
   'The Ballad of East and West' 20
Kirkcaldy (Fife) 80
Klaus, H Gustav 138n23
   Ecology and the Literature of the British Left: The Red and the Green (joint editor) 139n28

Koestler, Arthur
   The Gladiators 63n3
Korda, Alexander 128
the Kremlin (Moscow) 54
Krupp, Bertha 51
Kubrick, Stanley 64, 128

Labour Government 1923 123
Labour Government 1929–31 95
Labour Party 10, 42, 95, 123
   see also Labourites 106
Lawrence, DH 132, 137
League of Nations 12, 37
Left Review 102, 103, 103n21, 121, 134
Lenin, Vladimir 25, 42, 63
Lermontov, Mikhail 54
Liberal Democrat 135
Liebknecht, Karl 21, 64
Lindsay, Maurice
   History of Scottish Literature 131n4
Linklater, Eric 133
Livingstone, David 30
London 11, 14, 17, 25, 39, 40, 41, 46, 55, 56, 57, 69, 70, 72, 127
   literary scene 14
Longueval (France) 46
Louverture, Toussaint 105
Lumsden, Alison 138n25
Luxemburg, Rosa 64
Lyall, Scott 138n26, 139n27
   The International Companion to Lewis Grassic Gibbon (editor) 134, 136n16

McCallum, Eileen 129
McCleery, Alistair
   The Porpoise Press 1922–39 73n4
McCulloch, Margery Palmer 139n27
   with Dunnigan, Sarah M, *A Flame in the Mearns* (editor) 134

Modernism and Nationalism: Literature and Society in Scotland 1918–1939 (editor) 71n3
Scottish Modernism and Its Contexts 1918–1959 71n3, 139n27
MacDiarmid, Hugh 71, 73, 98, 105, 111, 125, 132, 133
   A Drunk Man Looks at the Thistle 71
   Penny Wheep 71
   'Politicians' 120
   Sangshaw 71
   see also M'Diarmid, Hugh 71
MacDonald, Ramsay 95, 102, 123
MacGillivray, James Pittendrigh 105
Machu Picchu (Peru) 29
Mack, Douglas S
   Scottish Fiction and the British Empire 138n26
Mackenzie, Compton 72, 89, 119, 136
Mackie Academy (Stonehaven) 9
Maclaren, Ian
   Beside the Bonnie Brier Bush 90
McLaren, Moray
   Return to Scotland 111n22
Macpherson, Ian
   Shepherds' Calendar 73
Magellan, Ferdinand 36
Malcolm, William K 129n1, 130
Malraux, André 68
Malzahn, Manfred 133n9
Mannofield (Aberdeen) 10
Margolies, David 103n21
Martha of Bethany 118
Marx, Karl 25, 42, 63
Marxism 54, 66
   see also agitprop 103
   see also Marxist ideology and theory 107, 135
Marxist–Leninism 107
Mary Magdalene 118

Massingham, HJ 28
The Golden Age 29
Maxwell, William 9
Maya 27, 29, 34, 35, 48, 61
  see also pre-Columbian theocracies 35
Mayan New Empire 34
Mayan Old Empire 34
Mealmarket Hall (Aberdeen) 10
Means Test 96, 102
  see also Public Assistance Committee (PAC) 102
the Mearns (Aberdeenshire) 8, 15, 40, 46, 72, 73, 79, 80, 98, 112, 114, 116, 121, 128
  see also Howe o' the Mearns 46
Mégroz, RL 51
Melville, Herman 74
  Typee 74
Mesoamerica 28, 35
Mexico
  Mexican regions 35
  Mexican states 34
Middle East 3, 12, 13, 18, 19, 23, 33
Middleton, Rebecca 13
  see also Mitchell, Ray
Middleton, Robert 80
The Millgate Monthly 29
Milner, Ian 134n14
Mitchell, Daryll (son) 14, 128
Mitchell, George (brother) 8
  see also Gibbon, George 4
Mitchell, Isabella (grandmother) 4
Mitchell, Jack 134n14
Mitchell, James Leslie
  criticism on his work 129–39
  ideas
    cosmopolitanism 122
    diffusionism 26, 28–9, 124
    humanitarianism 23, 41, 51–2, 53–4, 57–8, 59–60, 61–3, 66–7, 82, 104–6, 120–2, 135–6

literary influences 18, 34, 41, 49, 52, 54, 55, 65–6, 70, 72–4, 116
Littérature Engagée 102
love of nature 6, 37, 52, 55, 57, 74, 106–9, 110–1, 113, 114–5, 121, 139–40
magical realism 18, 50, 53
as a modernist 77–8, 125, 133, 134, 138–9
narrative method 18, 19, 20, 23, 31, 53, 60, 65, 74–9, 84–5, 98–9, 99–100, 109, 112, 117, 118–9, 121–2, 134
  see also heteroglossic narrative 76n7, 117
  see also intertextuality 44, 88
  see also narrative focalisation 57, 74, 85, 98, 133, 139
  see also polyphonic voice 31, 79
nihilism 40, 46–7, 54, 67–8
pacifism 11
personal mythology 6
political radicalism 6–8, 10–14, 20–1, 26–7, 30, 40, 41–2, 45–6, 54, 56, 64–5, 66–7, 97, 102–4, 117, 120, 122, 123, 125
post-colonialist revisionism 89, 124, 138
proto-feminism 44-5, 51, 55–7, 109–11, 139
social realism 40, 43, 80–4, 85–6, 94–6, 112, 114, 115
socialist utopianism 21
  see also utopian idealism 50, 130
use of Scots 41, 72, 74–6, 117, 125
views on art and literature 1–2, 42–3, 47–8, 49–50, 58, 59–60, 79–80, 102–4, 121–2, 125

INDEX

life
- ancestry 3–4
- parentage 4–5
- birth 1
- childhood 7, 8, 120
- adolescence 3, 8–9
- schooling 2, 3, 5, 8–9
- journalism 9–11
- Army 12–13
- Airforce 13–14
- London 14
- Welwyn Garden City 15
- death and burial 15

media and stage representations 128–9

non-fiction articles
- 'The Diffusionist Heresy' 29

non-fiction books
- *The Conquest of the Maya* 25, 34–6
- *Hanno* 14, 25, 29–30
- *Nine Against the Unknown* (*Earth Conquerors*) 25, 36–7, 111

novels
- autofiction 39–48
- historical novel 63–8
- imaginative romances 49–58
  - *Gay Hunter* 49, 50, 54–8, 130
  - *Image and Superscription* 13, 43, 60–3, 130
  - *The Lost Trumpet* 50, 52–4, 128
  - *Spartacus* 13, 63–8, 127, 128, 130, 131, 132
  - *Stained Radiance* 12, 14, 39–43, 44, 106, 130
  - *The Thirteenth Disciple* 2, 6, 13, 14, 39, 43–8, 60, 61, 130, 132
  - *Three Go Back* 50–2, 54, 55

stories
- *The Calends of Cairo* (*Cairo Dawns*) 17, 19–21
- *Persian Dawns, Egyptian Nights* 18, 19, 22–3

Polychromata 14, 18, 19, 53, 65, 113
- 'Daybreak' 14
- 'Dienekes' Dream' 22
- 'East is West' 20, 21
- 'Gift of the River' 14, 21
- 'It is Written' 21
- 'The Lost Prophetess' 20, 21
- 'Revolt' 22
  - see also 'One Man with a Dream' 22
- 'Siva Plays the Game' 19
- 'A Volcano in the Moon' 21

see also Gibbon, Lewis Grassic

Mitchell, James McIntosh (father) 3, 4, 6, 7, 8, 80
Mitchell, John (brother) 69
  see also Gibbon, John 4
Mitchell, Ray (wife) 14, 69, 72, 80, 127, 128
Mitchell, Rhea Sylvia (daughter) 14
  see also Martin, Rhea 128
Mitchison, Naomi 72, 133
  Black Sparta 66
  The Conquered 66
  The Corn King and the Spring Queen 66
  The Delicate Fire 66
Moll Flanders (Defoe) 75
Mondynes (Aberdeenshire) 112
Montrose (Angus) 96
Morley, Christopher 55
Morris, William 18, 21, 52
Moscow (Russia) 99
Muir, Edwin 125, 132
  Scottish Journey 111n22
  see also Muir, Edwin and Willa 72, 89
Munro, Ian S 128, 129, 136
Murray, Isobel 132
Mussolini, Benito 30, 58

Nanking Communists 106
Nansen, Fridtjof 27, 36, 37

INDEX

National Government 1931 95, 123
nationalism 2, 90
Nazism 90
  see also German Nazi Party 118
  see also Nazis 105
Neanderthalers 50
  see also Neanderthals 51
New Labour 135
New Women 44
Niger, river (Africa) 33
Nile, river (Egypt) 19
  see also Nile Valley 28
Norquay, Glenda 138n25
Norsemen 124
the Northeast (Scotland) 3, 73, 75, 81, 85, 109, 110, 111
North Sea 52, 123

Old Testament 53
Open University 130
Orwell, George 55, 58, 135
  Nineteen Eighty-Four 55
  see also Blair, Eric 135
O'Shaughnessy, Arthur
  'Ode' 22
Ottoman control in Egypt 13

Palenque (Mexico) 60, 62
Palestine 12
Pan Books (publisher) 128
Paris 60
Park, Mungo 25, 27, 30–4, 36
Paton, John, MP 10
Pavlov, Ivan 58
peasantry 4, 5, 35, 121
  see also peasant 5, 6, 35
Penguin (publisher) 130
Perry, William J 28, 29
  The Growth of Civilisation 29
Persia (Iran) 18, 23
Peruvian history 29
Peruvian islands 53
Peter the Apostle 118
Pick, JB 131
Picts 124

Plutarch 63
Poland 134
Polish Ukraine 105
Polo, Marco 36
Poole, Adrian
  'Introduction', in *The Cambridge Companion to English Novelists* 137n20
The Porpoise Press (publisher) 30
Post Office Savings Bank (London) 127
Power, William
  Literature and Oatmeal 131
  My Scotland 111n22
  Scotland and the Scots 111n22
Presbyterianism 33
Prescott, WH
  History of the Conquest of Mexico 34
Priestley, JB 119
Proust, Marcel 74, 125
Pushkin, Alexander 54
Putkowski, Julian, and Sykes, Julian
  Shot at Dawn 88n11
the Pyramids (Egypt) 19

Queen Victoria 1

Ramadan 20
'Red Clydeside' 11
'The Red Flag' 42, 106
Reformation (Scottish) 124
the Reisk (Arbuthnott) 8, 80, 96
Remarque, Erich Maria 73
  All Quiet on the Western Front 74, 86
Revolution of 1920 (Iraq) 12
Revolutionary Writers of the World 103
  see also Writers' International 102, 103
Robinson Crusoe (Defoe) 75
Roman conquest of Gaul 62

Roman Republic 64, 65, 66
Romans 52, 124
Romantic poets 110
Rome 63, 65
Roosevelt, Franklin D 58
Rossetti, Dante Gabriel 52
Routledge (publisher) 111, 131
Royal Air Force (RAF) 13, 17, 25, 39, 40
Royal Army Service Corps (RASC) 12, 13, 132
Royal Literary Fund 128
Royle, Trevor
   The Macmillan Companion to Scottish Literature 132
Ruskin, John 18, 21
Russia 10, 20, 136
Russian Revolution 122

Said, Edward 124
Sallust 63
Sartre, Jean-Paul 67, 107
Saudi Arabia 23
Saul (Paul the Apostle) 118
Scotland 10, 15, 20, 70, 79, 89, 104, 105, 122, 124, 125, 127, 134, 135, 136
The Scots Magazine 112, 113, 114
Scott, Sir Walter 3, 65, 71, 137
Scottish Covenanters 15
   see also Covenanters 124
   see also Covenanting period 84
Scottish Enlightenment 72
The Scottish Farmer 10, 46
Scottish Home Service (BBC) 129
Scottish literary renaissance 73, 74
   see also Modern Scottish Literary Renaissance 70, 71, 130
   see also Scottish literary revival 89
Scottish literary tradition 71, 88, 90, 125, 131, 132, 133
Scottish National Party 90
Scottish nationalism 3, 122, 124

Scottish PEN Club 127
Scottish publishing 72
Second World War 51, 111
Shaw, Brent D
   Spartacus and the Slave Wars: A Brief History with Documents 63n3
Shelley, PB 52, 127
   'Adonais' 40
Shepherd, Ian
   Aberdeen and North-East Scotland 8n9
Shepherd, Nan
   The Quarry Wood 73
Shepherd's Bush (London) 17
Shetland 112
Shiach, Morag 139n27
Silone, Ignazio
   Fontamara 134
Smith, Charlie 81
Smith, David
   Socialist Propaganda in the Twentieth-Century British Novel 138
Smith, Grafton Elliot 28, 29
   The Diffusion of Culture 111
   Human History 29
Smith, James
   The Cambridge Companion to British Literature of the 1930s (editor) 138
Social Democratic Federation (SDF) 10
socialism 2, 45
Socialist Realism 26
the Somme (France) 46, 47, 62
Soviet Russia 10, 54
   see also Soviet Union 135
Soviet Writers' Congress 99
   see also Maxim Gorky et al., *Soviet Writers' Congress 1934* 99n18
Spain 136
Spanish conquistadors 34
   see also Spanish invasion 35

Spartacists 21, 105
  see also Spartakusbund
    (Spartacus League) 64
Spartacus 27, 42, 52, 62, 64, 65,
  100, 105, 106
Spence, Lewis 105
the Sphinx (Egypt) 19
Stalin, Joseph 54, 58, 63
Stalinism 135
Stalinist era 26
Stevenson, Robert Louis
  *The Strange Case of Dr Jekyll
    and Mr Hyde* 34
Stonehaven (Aberdeenshire) 9,
  80, 112, 114
Strathdon (Aberdeenshire) 4
Strauss, Barry
  The Spartacus War 63n3
Stuart, Prince Charles Edward
  124
Sturgeon, Nicola 1
Suez Canal (Egypt) 13
Swinburne, Charles 18
the Sykes–Picot Agreement
  12

TAG Theatre 129
Tales of the Arabian Nights 19
Tennyson, Alfred, Lord 52
Thatcherite government 135
'There is a Green Hill Far Away'
  (hymn) 113
Thomaneck, JKA 135n15
Thomson, George Malcolm 72,
  89
  The Re-Discovery of Scotland
    111n22
  Scotland: That Distressed Area
    111n22
TP's and Cassell's Weekly 17
Transjordan 12
Tressell, Robert
  *The Ragged Trousered
    Philanthropists* 134
Trônes Wood (France) 46
The Twentieth Century 29

UK Independence Party (UKIP)
  135
Union of the Crowns 124, 136
Union of the Parliaments 124,
  137
United Kingdom (UK) 10, 98
United Nations (UN) 5
United States (USA) 15, 50, 89,
  134

de Vaca, Cabeza 36
Vercingetorix 52
Victorian age 2, 18
Vikings 27

Wallace, William 15, 84, 125
War of Independence (Scottish)
  124
Watson, Roderick
  The Literature of Scotland
    132n8
Wells, HG 14, 17, 18, 25, 49, 55
Welsh, Irvine 75
Welwyn (Hertfordshire) 61
  Queen Victoria Hospital,
    Welwyn 15
Welwyn Garden City 15, 72,
  112
the West 3, 18, 33
Whalsay (Shetland) 112
Whidden, James
  *Monarchy and Modernity in
    Egypt* 21n2
Whig view of history 28
Whitfield, Peter 130
Williams, Raymond
  The Country and the City
    137
Wiltshire Downs (south-west
  England) 55, 56
Wittig, Kurt
  *The Scottish Tradition in
    Literature* 131n3
Wokingham (Berkshire) 72
Woolf, Virginia 74, 77
Wordsworth, William 110

Yeats, WB 136
Young, Douglas F
  Beyond the Sunset 73n5, 130
Yucatán 34, 61

Zaghloul, Saad 23
Zagratzki, Uwe 130
Zola, Emil
  The Earth 134

www.ingramcontent.com/pod-product-compliance
Lightning Source LLC
Chambersburg PA
CBHW051645230426
43669CB00013B/2450